Dear Teacher

1001 Teachable Moments for K–3 Classrooms

Martha Brady

Drawings by Michele Edwards

TEACHER IDEAS PRESS
Portsmouth, NH

For Emilie and Pat—M.B.

For my father—M.E.

Teacher Ideas Press
A division of Reed Elsevier Inc.
361 Hanover Street
Portsmouth, NH 03801
www.teacherideaspress.com

Offices and agents throughout the world

Library of Congress Cataloging-in-Publication Data

Brady, Martha.
    Dear Teacher : 1001 teachable moments for K-3 classrooms / by Martha Brady;
  drawings by Michele Edwards.
      p. cm.
    ISBN 1-59158-025-0
    1. Education, Primary-Activity programs. 2. Multiple intelligences.
  I. Title.
    LB1537 .B72 2003
    372.21—dc21   2003014282

Editor: Suzanne Barchers
Production Coordinator: Angela Laughlin
Typesetter: Westchester Book Services
Cover design: Joni Doherty
Manufacturing: Steve Bernier

08 07 06 05 04 VP 1 2 3 4 5

Contents

Acknowledgments

It is with gratitude and sincere appreciation that I acknowledge the people who were instrumental in moving this book project toward its completion. To my editor, Suzanne Barchers, who continues to support and pull out yet another book from me when I think I can't possibly have any more ideas skating around in that roller rink I call a brain, I thank you. You are a consummate professional and a good friend, and I so value both sides of that coin.

To my university students, too many to count, who continue to keep me present and grounded and aware that we learn from the heart as well as from the head, and especially to the Praxis students, many of whom allowed me to use their ideas on photography for this book, I salute you and honor your decision to become teachers. May your beacons light the way for those children who have lost theirs.

To my university colleagues Margaret, Peggy, Sally, Linda, and of course Emilie and Pat, who seamlessly perpetuate the notion that what I do and how I do it is worthy and will, in the long run, reap a harvest for which many children will benefit, I am eternally grateful to work in your circle.

A special thanks goes to the availability of the Arizona Department of Education's state standards that I used as guides for keeping me on track in the curricular arena.

To Michele and her wonderful child-centered artwork, thank you for letting me use that side of your brain to create a sense of visual wonder and awe for some teachers and kids whose names we will never know.

And finally, to the authors of the many children's books I cite in this book and use as catalysts for child-centered experiences, I honor your art and craft.

Introduction

Dear Teacher,

In putting this latest book together, I have tried diligently to make it as straightforward, simple, and to the point as possible. Hopefully, I have created and collected an array of learning experiences for your primary students offering strong choices for creative expression in a sequential, substantive manner.

Each chapter is formatted very cleanly and gives you an opportunity to connect the different aspects of these lessons into one whole lesson that allows your boys and girls to delve into their own understanding of the arts, a strong use of their five senses, and, most importantly, a chance to choose how to make meaning for themselves and to reflect upon that meaning.

Based on commonly required academic standards for K–3 students, the chapters in this book follow the outline that is described below.

Dear Teacher

Each chapter begins with an introductory letter to the reader, introducing the designated topic or unit for that particular chapter. This letter may include definitions of the topic, simple lead-in activities for the chapter, chants, poems, resource book suggestions, children's literature suggestions, personal experiences relating to the topic at hand, or even rhymes, riddles, clues, or song lyrics. The introductory letter sets the tone and offers the reader a jumpstart to the activities that are included in the chapter.

Teachable Moments

After the introductory Dear Teacher letters, the chapters begin with whimsical paragraphs that offer personal events or experiences similar to those from which *teachable moments* are born. For lack of a better word, they are mini history lessons, moments in time that can bring about other moments in time.

Activities

Each chapter includes a selection of K–3 activities that are broken down into the following categories:

Content: This category defines the curricular area or areas that are being addressed in the particular activity.

Lesson: This category is the title of the specific lesson being presented. It gives the reader a clue to the central focus of the intended experience.

Standards: This category describes the specific academic standards or teaching requirements being covered. This particular aspect of the lesson breakdown shows the overall purpose for the teaching of the lesson and the foundation from which the lesson arises.

Multiple Intelligences: This category highlights the appropriate multiple intelligences that are covered with the teaching of this particular lesson. This author uses Howard Gardner's theory of multiple intelligences as the core for almost all of the ideas, strategies, and experiences in this book. Giving children an entry into their own capacities for making meaning of any kind of lesson may possibly create the structure for success in students' efforts. Therefore, lessons incorporate Verbal/ Linguistic (writing, listening, speaking), Logical/Mathematical (concepts, patterns, relationships, numbers), Bodily/Kinesthetic (manipulatives, construction, use of body), Musical/Rhythmic (rhythm and melody), Visual/ Spatial (images, pictures, color consciousness), Interpersonal (interactions, cooperation, relationships), Intrapersonal (self-awareness), and Naturalist (environment) learning experiences.

Materials: A list of materials and supplies needed for the success of a particular lesson is included in this category.

Grade Level: This important category shows teachers the appropriate age level of the intended lesson even though most of the activities can be adapted to fit most learning levels.

Objective: This explains the intention of the lesson. Each objective will be written in observable terms. That is, experiences the students undertake can be seen or observed so that accurate assessment can be ascertained.

Before: This beginning segment is the groundwork for each lesson. It sets the framework, brings out a student's prior knowledge of the subject and/or topic, and offers students a first taste of what is yet to come.

First: This segment awakens the students' interests (Lazear, 1991*), and offers a way for students to focus on or get hooked to the lesson. This part of the lesson is the initial or first connection experience with the lesson at hand.

Next: This segment amplifies interest (Lazear, 1991) and creates an event in which children can begin to make some sense of what is about to be taught. That is, students are given a second chance to "engage" in the lesson. Imagine a pebble thrown into a pond. This segment begins the "ring of water."

Then: In most instances, this is the lesson to be taught. The experiences in this segment generally are planned toward meeting the objective. This segment is the part of the lesson that uses one or two intelligences as a means of having children make meaning.

Finally: This segment usually ends the lesson with some type of reflective experience, either individually or as a group, and is an experience that connects the lesson to the students' own lives to some degree.

Alternative Assessment: This segment offers assessment tools that allow students to show what they know in unique ways rather than by traditional pencil-and-paper methods.

Toward the end of each chapter, four more segments are added as a way of giving the reader even more experiences with which to engage children. These last four wrap-up segments are as follows:

*Lazear, David. *Seven Ways of Teaching,* Palatine, IL: IRI/Skylight Publishing, 1991.

And Now, What about That One Good Book and Those Five Good Lessons?

This segment uses a current or classic children's book and creates five curricular lessons that relate to the contents of the book.

Oh Yes, Remember the Teachable Moment?

This segment includes one activity stemming from the teachable moment paragraph at the beginning of each chapter.

A Picture Is Worth a Thousand Words

The activities in this particular segment integrate the art drawing found in each chapter and give students an opportunity to use visual spatial capacities to demonstrate a specific understanding of the lesson or lessons.

Grids

Two grids of forty ideas each, geared specifically toward grades K–3 and grades 4–6, are created to categorize the teaching ideas into the appropriate multiple intelligence blocks.

I've been at this teaching thing for a long time and have yet to be disappointed in my ability to teach when I open myself up to what my mind continues to give me or what other minds lend me for the purpose of changing the lives of some children.

I'm lending this book to you for the purpose of doing just that; perhaps, for a moment, changing the way one child learns, or sees, or understands, or feels, or grasps, or owns, or breathes in the day. That is all.

.

BUGS

Dear Teacher,

I know a lot about bugs and spiders. I know that stepping on them in the middle of the night as I grope my way to the bathroom is not one of the highlights of my existence. I know that sitting in my living room with friends and watching something with more legs than the New York City Rockettes slide across the coffee table does not make for the conversation I intended.

I know that anything that can hide in my shoe without asking permission first is really not offering the kind of relationship I wish to nurture and further along.

I also know that kids love bugs. They love things that squirm and crawl and slither and sneak. They love things that flatten and roll into balls and climb and hang. They love things that make Mother spend quality time standing on a kitchen chair. They simply love critters and creatures that belong in a sci-fi movie.

This chapter is full of ideas you can bring into the classroom for just that purpose. Not to make Mom stand on a chair or to create a teacher's guide for the movie *Alien*, but to continue to nurture the love affair between bugs and children. To help that along, *The Best Book of Bugs* (New York: King Fisher, 1998), a marvelous illustrative text by Claire Llewllyn, and James K. Wangberg's *Do Bees Sneeze* (Golden, CO: Fulcrum Publishing, 1997), a book brimming with questions that kids ask about insects, are but two excellent resource books that will offer hours of enjoyment and information gathering for your students.

In my capacity as a university professor who is lucky to go into classrooms on a daily basis, I see many, many bug drawings and I hear many, many bug stories. This is one is my favorite stories and a perfect way to get us into this chapter on bugs.

One day, not long ago, I went into a second-grade classroom to observe one of my university students and to simply see the action of 7-year-olds. I sat down by a young girl and quite simply said, "Tell me something about bugs that you know a lot about." Fifteen enthralling minutes later, I walked out of the room and wondered why all learning could not be as rich, as connected, and as alive as knowing everything there is to know about ladybugs.

You think of yourself as an early riser, the smell of morning coffee an olfactory umbilical cord that tugs you out of your warm, cozy, cave of a bed. You step onto the soft, fuzzy carpet and notice that your two cats are standing, ceramic-like, seemingly saluting a small shadow that is lingering, imperceptively, inside your bedroom slipper. You bend down to give the shadow a name, and suddenly you scream a scream of which the entire cast of Halloween, Part VI *would be immeasurably proud.*

Out skitters a scorpion, tail bent like an ornate wrought iron bookend holding Harry Potter at attention. You look at the two cats in total disgust, and then a somewhat panicked smile slides across your face. And in an instant, you have the makings of a brilliant lesson on bugs. A teachable moment has crept into your life, and you are ever so pleased.

Activity 1

Content: Language Arts

Lesson: Creative Writing

Standard: Using descriptive words to write a creative story, which has a beginning, middle, and end.

Multiple Intelligences: Verbal/Linguistic: Students will practice the order and meaning of words. Visual/Spatial: Students will create graphic representations.

Materials: Icky bug, butcher paper, art paper, markers, resource books on insects

Grade Level: 3+

Objective: The students will brainstorm common nouns, verbs, proper nouns, and original onomatopoeic words relating to insects and/or spiders. The students will use some of those words to create an original story about a personal encounter with an insect or spider.

Before: Create an "icky" bug out of a Styrofoam ball, pipe cleaners, tissue paper, and other materials. Place it on a table in front of the class where students can see it. On the board, write the letters of the alphabet. Students will look at the icky bug and call out words that describe that bug. They will write those words in the appropriate spaces next to the appropriate letters of the alphabet.

First: In groups, students will use large pieces of butcher paper to create ongoing ABC resource lists of common nouns, proper nouns, verbs, and onomatopoeic words relating to bugs, spiders, and insects. Examples using many of the letters of the alphabet may include:

Common Nouns

a—antenna	**b**—bee	**c**—compound eye
d—drone	**e**—exoskeleton	**f**—fleas
g—gyroscope	**h**—head	**i**—insecticides
j—juice	**k**—known species	**l**—larva

m—mandible **n**—nectar **o**—oxygen

p—proboscis **q**—queen **r**—regeneration

s—swarms **t**—thorax **u**—ultraviolet light

v—veins **w**—wings

Proper Nouns

a—Anopheles **b**—Bombadier beetle **c**—Culex mosquito

d—Drone fly **e**—Electric-light bug **f**—Firefly beetle

g—Gypsy moth **h**—Honeybee **i**—Io moth

j—Jesus bug **k**—Katydid **l**—Ladybug beetle

m—Monarch butterfly **n**—Nepa **o**—Orb-weave spider

p—Promethea caterpillar **q**— **r**—Red-legged grasshopper

s—Sphinx moth **t**—Tarantula **u**—Uknobbed moth

v—Viceroy butterfly **w**—Whirligig beetle

Verbs

a—attack **b**—bite **c**—chew

d—dive **e**—examine **f**—feed

g—grasp **h**—hatch **i**—incubate

j—jump **k**—kiss **l**—live

m—mimic **n**—nourish **o**—outgrow

p—produce **q**—quench **r**—race

s—stings **t**—tunnels **u**—

v— **w**—waggle

Onomatopoeic Words

buzz hiss crunch

splat swarm snap

crink boing dwop

plop skitter pop

clatter swat creep

smush whir

Next: Pairing off, one student will select one or two words from each list. Using these words, that student will describe or retell personal bug stories, fact or fiction. As these stories are being described or retold, the other student will draw what is being heard or imagined.

Then: Students will take the bug drawings they made from hearing someone else's story, give the bugs an original name, and write an original story of that bug's life, complete with a beginning, middle, and end.

Finally: The teacher will show several slides or pictures of dust mites and ask students to use three words to describe each picture. The creative writing stories and the illustrations will then be collected and made into a class book to be used later as a catalyst for lessons focusing on similarities/differences, prediction, habitat, and fact and fiction.

Alternative Assessment: Students will use class resource books or go to the library to research actual insects and/or spiders that have similar characteristics to the "made-up" bug, and then present the information to the class through writing, telling, or drawings.

Activity 2

Content: Language Arts

Lesson: Point of View

Standard: Write a report that conveys a point of view and develops a topic with appropriate facts, details, examples, and descriptions.

Multiple Intelligences: Visual/Spatial: Students will use active imagination and image manipulation. Verbal/Linguistic: Students will use memory and recall.

Materials: Copies of newspaper articles, music, magnifying glasses

Grade Level: 3+

Objective: Students will use an imagery experience to write a point of view newspaper account of an insect sighting.

Before: Review the 5 W's of writing a newspaper article: who, what, when, where, and why. Make copies of two articles found in a newspaper. Students will locate the who, what, when, where, and why of those articles and discuss the similarities of the 5 W's in those articles.

First: Darken the room, play some soft music, then take the boys and girls on the following practice imagery experience:

> I want everyone to close your eyes right now. I am going to tell you a story and as I do, I want you to follow along and try to picture things in your mind as I tell the story. . . . Are you ready? Here we go.
>
> You are standing in front of the front door to your house or apartment. Please pretend to put your hand on the doorknob of your front door. Now, open the door . . . and walk through all the rooms that you have to walk through in order to get to your bedroom. . . . Walk to your bedroom and sit on the corner of your bed. Now, in your mind, notice one thing you can see in your room if you are sitting on the corner of your bed. When I say 1-2-3, you will open your eyes and I will ask you what you see. One, two, three.

Then: Students will describe one object or item they can see while sitting on the corner of their beds.

Next: The students will get in a comfortable position as the following imagery story is told:

> We are on our way to the airport. We are in a school bus, heading toward the airport. Look, we are getting closer and closer to the airport. I see many planes landing and taking off. I see many planes parked next to the gates of the airport. We get off the bus and go into

the airport terminal. A man walks up and welcomes us to the airport and tells us to follow him. He leads us to a gate and guides us down a ramp to the open door of a plane. We walk in, then walk down the aisle of the plane to find our seats. The plane hurls down the runway and lifts off. We are flying high in the air. Soon, the copilot tells us that we must now put on our parachutes. We put them on, tight and snug. He then opens the door of the plane and one by one, we bail out. Down, down, down we float, through the clouds, toward the ground. As we get closer and closer, we notice that we are going to land in a grassy field. As our feet touch the ground, our bodies begin to shrink. Smaller and smaller we become. We become so small that the blades of grass begin to resemble towering trees. Slowly we sink to the ground, surrounded by the tall, tall blades of grass. When we land, we take off our parachutes and begin walking through and around the blades of grass. We see a small twig that looks as large as a tree trunk. We crawl under it to get to the other side. Suddenly, we hear a loud noise. We walk a bit further, and there right in front of us is a large insect. We hide behind a giant leaf until we decide what to do next. When I count to three, open your eyes. One, two, three.

Then: Students will use this imagery experience to write a point of view account of the encounter with the bug. Students will select their own point of view.

Finally: Students will discuss the aspects of the imagery that were the most vivid to them. Students will also think about and discuss this reflective question: "How did the imagery experience help you with the writing of your point of view article?"

Alternative Assessment: Children will go outside with magnifying glasses, find an insect, and tell a point of view story of that insect as the rest of the class looks at the insect in question.

Activity 3

Content: Math

Lesson: Logic

Standard: Use *if* and *then* statements to construct simple, valid arguments.

Multiple Intelligences: Logical/Mathematical: Students will discern relationships and connections. Visual/Spatial: Students will create representative images.

Materials: Insect pictures, butterfly pictures, illustrated insect resource books, pipe cleaners, paper rolls, glitter, colored tissue paper, markers, glue, construction paper

Grade Level: 3+

Objective: Students will construct bugs and use them as objects for answering *if* and *then* statements.

Before: Show a photo with a collection of butterflies on it. Ask students to answer this question, "ALL of the butterflies _____." Examples may include:

All of the butterflies are dead.

All of the butterflies have wings.

All of the butterflies have antennae.

First: Show several pictures of different insects including moths, beetles, bees, butterflies, mites, flies, dragonflies, silverfish, katydids, ladybugs, gnats, and crickets. Discuss the different and similar characteristics.

Next: Students will use paper towel rolls, pipe cleaners, tissue paper, buttons, yarn, glitter, and other materials to create an insect.

Then: Students will place the collection of bugs on a table. While looking at the entire group of bugs, students will answer the following statements:

> *All* of the bugs _____.
>
> *Every* bug _____.
>
> *Some* of the bugs _____.
>
> *None* of the bugs _____.
>
> *Many* of the bugs _____.
>
> *More than half* of the bugs _____.
>
> *Almost all* of the bugs _____.
>
> *If* all the bugs were dangerous looking, *then* _____.

Finally: Relate the above statements to the students in the class. Have the class look around the room and at each other and answer the following:

> *All* of the students in this class _____.
>
> *Some* of the students in this class _____.
>
> *None* of the students in this class _____.
>
> *Many* of the students in this class _____.
>
> *More than half* of the students in this class _____.
>
> *Almost all* of the students in this class _____.
>
> *If* all of the students in this class were _____, *then* _____.

Alternative Assessment: Students will select an assortment of like objects in the classroom (books, desks, coats, pencils, backpacks) and answer the above *if/then* statements relating to the chosen objects.

Activity 4

Content: Science

Lesson: Characteristics of Insects

Standard: Identify characteristics of plants and animals.

Multiple Intelligence: Musical/Rhythmic: Students will sing an existing melody.

Materials: *The Icky Bug Alphabet Book* by Jerry Pallotta; transparency or copies of the "There's an Ant That's Crawling Up My Leg" lyrics; tape of the song, "She'll Be Comin' 'Round the Mountain; tape of the song, "Itsy Bitsy Spider"; overhead transparency of "Itsy Bitsy Spider"; "word catcher"

Grade Level: 2+

Objective: Students will sing songs as a way of reviewing or learning about the characteristics of certain insects. Students will write song lyrics that include five facts about bugs.

Before: Review the common parts of an insect (wings, proboscis, compound eye, thorax, scales, antennae, sensory hairs, mandible, and so on). Show pictures of insects with these labeled parts. Also, review and compare the differences between moths and butterflies.

First: Read Jerry Pallotta's *The Icky Bug Alphabet Book.* Discuss different characteristics of insects.

Next: Students will choose one insect from Pallotta's book and create a rap, chant, or song. "She'll Be Comin' 'Round the Mountain" is a good melody for children to use as they create original lyrics. A simple format such as the one below works well when children begin to write lyrics for the first time.

> There's an ant that's *crawling* up my leg.
>
> There's an ant that's *crawling* up my leg.
>
> There's an ant that's *crawling,* now he's started *stinging.*
>
> There's an ant that's *crawling* up my leg.
>
> There's a mantis *staring* straight at me.
>
> There's a mantis *staring* straight at me.
>
> There's a mantis *staring,* now he's started *praying.*
>
> There's a mantis *staring* straight at me.

Students may also sing the following song, "The Busy, Busy Beetle," to the tune of "Itsy Bitsy Spider."

The Busy, Busy Beetle

> The busy, busy beetle
> crawls on the forest floor.
> It munches and it nibbles
> and always looks for more.
> Some eat little creature snacks
> and some just like a salad.
> But all this eating helps the soil
> and that's a fact that's valid.
> And then there is the butterfly.
> Please don't forget the moth.
> One is busy in the day,
> one likes night a lot.
> The wings of both have tiny scales
> that shimmer as they fly.
> If I could metamorphasize
> I'd give this all a try.

Then: Use a "word catcher" (a small, square piece of poster board with an attached handle) to catch some of the facts found in the lyrics of the song. Simply take the word catcher and hold it over selected facts in the lyrics that are projected on the screen from the overhead. Pull the word catcher out toward you. This will enlarge the word on the screen and give the impression of catching the word in midair. Have students find different facts stated in the lyrics and "catch them."

Children will use the tune of "Itsy Bitsy Spider" to create their own lyrics. Make sure they include five facts about insects in their original lyrics.

Finally: Students will answer this question: "Why does music make it easier to remember facts?"

Alternative Assessment: Students will teach their song with the new lyrics to the class. Other students will point out the correct facts imbedded in the lyrics.

Activity 5

Content: Science, Language Arts

Lesson: Habitat

Standard: Identify characteristics of bugs that allow them to live in specific environments and habitats.

Multiple Intelligence: Verbal/Linguistic: Students will explain what they have learned. They will understand the order and meaning of words.

Materials: Art supplies and materials, resource books, white butcher paper, white precut poster board strips

Grade Level: 3+

Objective: Students will research a specific insect or spider, create the insect or spider from classroom materials, and draw an appropriate habitat in which to place the insect or spider.

Before: Take the students outside and have them look for natural habitats of insects or spiders. Have them place this information into their science journals. If the boys and girls keep science field sketch journals as well, have them add these findings in sketch form to that journal, complete with field notes.

First: Students will select and research one type of insect or spider and the habitat in which that insect or spider lives.

Next: Students will create the insect or spider from classroom materials, place each insect on a long piece of white butcher paper that has been taped onto a table, and draw the appropriate habitat around the assigned insect or spider. Students will also label significant aspects of the habitat.

Then: Students will select someone else's insect/spider habitat drawing and use this information to create a piece of writing relating to that specific habitat. The writing piece may include a poem, a factual account, a point of view narrative, another song lyric, a riddle, and so on.

Finally: Students will compare their own home environments with the environment they created for their assigned insect or spider. Comparative questions may include:

1. How does each environment keep its occupant safe from weather?
2. How do both environments affect each other positively or negatively?
3. How is everyday existence similar in both environments?

Alternative Assessment: Students will create a collection of five bookmarks, each including facts about one certain insect or spider, and one illustrative drawing of that insect. Bookmarks will be laminated and either used on a daily basis or given as gifts to another classroom.

✓ *And now, what about five good lessons from one good book?* See if these work.

The book: Shields, Carol Diggory. Illustrated by Scott Nash. (2002). *The Buggliest Bug.* Cambridge, MA: Candlewick Press.

1. On the inside cover of *The Buggliest Bug* sit two bugs in tall, tall grass. Students will invent a conversation they think is taking place between the two bugs.
2. Students will research inventions and/or medicine that have some direct connection to insects of some type. Students will create a timeline of that connection.
3. Look at the bug fact cards in the back of the book. Students will choose one of the bugs in the story and create their own bug comic strips. Have students use rulers to draw an eight-cell strip on paper, and then create a sequential, imaginative story about the selected bug. At least one true fact about the bug should be included in the comic strip.
4. Students will use illustrations of this book and other books to show how illustrators draw bugs differently and what aspect of the bug each illustrator focuses on, such as the head, the eyes, the feet, the movement, and so on.
5. The class will hold its own "buggliest bug" contest. Students will bring in bugs of all sorts (in containers, of course). Each contestant will become the expert on his or her bug. Prizes for the scariest, the prettiest, the biggest, the fastest, the most interesting, and the stupidest will be given.

✓ *Oh yes. Remember the teachable moment* that introduced our activities in this chapter? Well, here is a little lesson to go with that idea.

Activity 6

Content: Science

Lesson: Defense Mechanisms in Insects

Standards: Students will identify cause-effect relationships in living systems. Students will describe the functions of basic animal structures.

Multiple Intelligence: Verbal/Linguistic: Students will teach others on the computer.

Materials: Computer

Grade Level: 3+

Objective: Students will research poisonous insects and arachnids on the Internet.

Before: Lead a discussion with students about close encounters with poisonous insects and/or arachnids.

First: Log onto www.desertusa.com and take a brief lesson on scorpions.

Next: Log onto Koday's Kids Amazing Insects, http://www.ivyhall.district96.k12.il.us/4th/kkhp/1insects/bugmenu.html. Students will select one of the age-appropriate activities found on this web site.

Then: Students will create a list of questions they wish to ask the pen pal.

Finally: Students will use what they have learned from the pen pal to present a joint presentation with the pen pal via the Internet or a solo presentation.

Alternative Assessment: Use facts gathered from the presentations to play Bug Jeopardy.

✔ And finally, if you think *a picture is worth a thousand words,* use the drawing of this magnificent praying mantis above to engage your students in seeing, writing, drawing, or just thinking about bugs, spiders, or creepy crawlers in general. The following activities will work wonders for those students in your classroom who simply understand the life of bugs and all things icky if they are given the chance to make meaning by seeing in color, shape, form, and design.

Activity 7

Content: Science

Lesson: Habitats

Standard: Students will identify characteristics of plants and animals that allow them to live in specific environments.

Multiple Intelligences: Visual/Spatial: Students will use a visual drawing as a stimulus. Logical/Mathematical: Students will make comparisons.

Materials: Copies of the praying mantis drawing

Grade Level: 3

Objective: Students will use factual information to create habitats. Students will compare habitats.

Before: Students will look at the praying mantis drawing and label the parts of the insect that are familiar to them.

First: Give each child two copies of the praying mantis drawing. Students will use one copy to draw a habitat surrounding this praying mantis that is *not* factual.

Next: Students will share their new habitats with the rest of the class and discuss the information they know to be true about praying mantises and why, with this information, their particular habitats would not work for the praying mantis.

Then: With the other copy of the drawing, students will draw an actual true habitat for the praying mantis. Again, using information they know about praying mantises, students will discuss why this particular habitat works.

Finally: Students will reflect upon the "habitat" of the classroom and compare it to that of the praying mantis.

Alternative Assessment: Students will research the praying mantis and label the remaining parts of the insect not labeled at the beginning of the lesson.

Activity 8

Content: Science, Arts

Lesson: Creative Writing

Standards: Students will write an original paragraph or story. Students will select and use subjects in works of art.

Multiple Intelligences: Visual/Spatial: Students will draw a mural. Verbal/Linguistic: Students will write. Naturalist: Students will research factual information about the environment.

Materials: Copies of the praying mantis drawing

Grade Level: 2–3

Objective: Students will create a community mural and use the mural as a stimulus for a creative writing activity.

Before: Students will use a long piece of butcher paper to draw a large forest environment.

First: Students will color their own copies of the praying mantis drawing, cut them out, and find places to hide them on the mural of the forest environment.

Next: Students will use the mural, complete with the praying mantises, to write an original paragraph or story about what they see, or they may wish to write a paragraph giving clues as to where their own particular praying mantises may be hidden.

Then: Students will add any drawings to the mural representing what was described in their own stories.

Finally: Students will share stories, discuss the mural as a whole, and reflect upon their own appreciation of others' work.

Alternative Assessment: Students will add one drawing to the mural that is factual. Students will then label all aspects of the mural, researching drawings on the mural first if they are unfamiliar with the factual name, definition, and so on of a particular drawing.

Activity 9

Content: Science, Math

Lesson: True or False Problem Solving

Standard: Students will understand that science involves asking and answering questions and comparing results to what is known.

Multiple Intelligences: Logical/Mathematical: Students will solve problems. Verbal/Linguistic: Students will answer questions.

Materials: Resource materials, transparency of praying mantis drawing

Grade Level: 3

Objective: Students will research information regarding the praying mantis. Students will make visual additions to an existing drawing of a praying mantis representing answers to questions that were asked.

Before: Make an overhead transparency of the praying mantis drawing or use an opaque machine to enlarge the drawing and place it on a bulletin board.

First: Students will use the Internet, library, or in-class resource books to research one or two questions about the life cycle of the praying mantis and its habitat. They will write down the questions on a 5" × 7" card and the resources from which the questions came.

Next: The class will observe the overhead transparency or enlarged drawing of the praying mantis as they ask each other the researched questions about the praying mantis. When questions are answered correctly, either the writer of the question or the student who answers can go to the overhead or bulletin board and draw something onto the existing drawing that represents the correct answer.

Then: Students will make concluding statements about the final drawing and the research information gathered. Some suggested concluding statements may begin with:

1. One thing I learned about the praying mantis is _____.
2. I was unaware that the praying mantis _____.
3. I was surprised to find out that the praying mantis _____.
4. I still don't get how the praying mantis _____.
5. The thing about a praying mantis that I find so hard to believe is _____.
6. Praying mantises scare me because _____.
7. The most important fact about a praying mantis that I've learned is _____.
8. Praying mantises remind me of _____ because _____.
9. I wish to learn more about how the praying mantis _____.
10. The one question about praying mantises I still want to know the answer to is _____.

Finally: Students will reflect upon question #8, "Praying mantises remind me of _____ because _____." This reflective component can be accomplished through discussion, writing, sculpting with clay, or drawing.

Alternative Assessment: Students will rewrite research questions about the praying mantis, collate the written questions, and put them into fact books for future use.

Activity 10

Content: Language Arts

Lesson: Telling Stories

Standard: Students will use effective vocabulary and organization to relate information.

Multiple Intelligences: Visual/Spatial: Students will use the praying mantis drawing as a stimulus for telling a story. Verbal/Linguistic: Students will tell a story. Intrapersonal: Students will reflect upon past experiences.

Materials: Copies of the praying mantis drawing

Grade Level: K–3

Objective: Students will look at the different elements of the drawing in this chapter and tell an original story.

Before: Students will review important aspects of telling a story.

First: Students will use the praying mantis drawing as a stimulus for telling stories about different experiences happening in the scenes in the picture.

Next: Students will relate personal stories that correspond to the original stories being told.

Then: Students will answer "What would happen if…" questions about the picture.

Finally: Students will reflect upon their own appreciation of the drawing.

Alternative Assessment: Students will take a drawing home and ask a family member to tell them a story that comes from viewing the drawing.

To wrap up this chapter, here is every idea you ever wanted to know about bugs! Perhaps a good bug story is the perfect way to begin a *creepy, crawly* day in the classroom.

Bugs K–3

V/L	Read Jerry Pallotta's *The Icky Bug Alphabet Book*.	Write about the ickiest bug you know.	Use bug names to create riddles; e.g., How does a horse fly? "Tell me one thing Katy did."	To create an ABC book, interview family members about personal interactions with bugs.	Write a story about why ants always stay in a straight line.
L/M	Make comparisons between a firefly and a light bulb.	Use a computer to create fact cards about bugs.	Create a chart comparing characteristics of moths and butterflies.	Create a KWL chart on spiders.	Explore patterns found on butterfly, moth, and dragonfly wings.
V/S	Create "Ants on a Log" with celery, raisins, and peanut butter. Draw a habitat for the ants.	Create a large natural mural on which to place all kinds of homemade insects.	Use pipe cleaners to create three dimensional bugs. Pin on the background mural.	Illustrate your own ABC Bug Book.	Create an imagery that takes children to the rain forest.
B/K	Build an ant farm for the classroom.	Create a game about bugs using the fact cards.	Use string to outline or "grid" a square foot of ground. Study the bug culture in that area.	In groups, build a habitat or diorama for one specific kind of insect or spider.	Pantomime characteristics of different types of insects. Play "bug charades."
M/R	Create a four-line chant about an icky bug or spider of choice.	Sing the "Bug Song." Create new lyrics.	Listen to nature sound effects. Use these sounds as a writing or discussion stimulus.	Create a spider song using the tune "Three Blind Mice."	Create a call/response chant to use for reviewing insects.
Inter	Teach the class one thing you discovered in your bug culture grid.	Turn to a partner and recall facts about ants during the process of building an ant farm.	Teach the class how to play your game.	Brainstorm methods for exhibiting the habitats in the classroom or library.	With a partner, research insects or spiders whose bites are harmful.
Intra	Draw your response of "why grasshoppers hop."	Talk about "why some bugs are icky to you."	Journal about your most "terrible bug experience."	"Close your eyes and think about having compound eyes. Why would that be a good thing, or not?"	"Choose one way to tell the teacher every thing you know about one kind of insect."
N	Show how monarch butterflies survive their migration patterns.	Research the life expectancy of bugs. Create a chart categorizing reasons for their demise.	Show and tell the basic differences between insects and spiders.	Learn the names of several body parts of an insect.	Compare these insect body parts to your own.

The activities and experiences in this grid are just a bit more difficult and can bring some challenges to your students. These ideas can be used as extension lessons or individual projects, or, in some cases, in learning centers.

Bugs 4–6

V/L	Write an original children's book about insects that are now extinct.	Create a "goose bump" story about an insect or spider. Put it on a cassette tape.	Write myth/fact cards about spiders and insects. Create a class file.	Read the completed original books to children in primary grades.	Keep a science diary of insects or spiders you observe during a period of time.
L/M	Create a cause/effect chart of insect devastation around the world.	Create a timetable of significant events insects played in history.	Research and collect species of five different orders of insects. Show in a categorized way.	Keep an ongoing count of butterflies sighted during a monthlong period.	Chart this data.
V/S	Find a good-sized picture of an insect of choice. Cut it in half. Glue one side on art paper. Draw the "missing" side.	Use tactile objects to illustrate this book.	Draw the life cycle of one particular insect or spider.	Preview a fictionalized movie about insects or spiders. Show it in class.	Draw and label the "perfect" insect that would benefit humanity.
B/K	Use a magnifying glass to find hidden insects in grass.	Create a "bug catcher" for a specific bug.	Choose one insect or spider. Create a board game of facts and figures about that insect or spider.	Create a Listening Center using a collection of these original cassette tapes.	Act out this life cycle.
M/R	Create a rap as a way of explaining the life cycle of a certain insect.	Bring a song about insects or spiders to class and teach it to the rest of the students.	Create a tape of "night sounds." Use as background music for cassette tape Listening Center.	Use an existing tune to create new lyrics including a set number of factual or fictional information.	Bring "junk" items to class. Use these items to duplicate the "night sounds."
Inter	Be an expert on one insect. Teach a lesson about that insect to the rest of the class.	With a partner write a user's manual for this new product.	Make a presentation to the class regarding the scientific errors found in the movie.	Interview scientists, exterminators, or other experts to collect data for the class presentation.	Volunteer to bring an expert to class for a class discussion. Set up discussion agenda.
Intra	Observe the same insect or spider for a week. Keep a journal whose entries begin with "I wonder."	Reflect on the question, "What bugs you about bugs?"	Think about and share ways that insects or spiders help the life of your family.	Do an independent research project on poisonous insects or spiders.	Do an independent research project on the silk industry.
N	Show how certain insects communicate with each other.	Give a report on the use of insects and/or spiders in medical research.	Create an insect adaptability mobile.	Learn the scientific names of the different orders of insects. Research some of these orders.	Research how insects affect the farming industry positively or negatively.

CATS AND DOGS

Dear Teacher,

"Cats may exasperate. They may not come when called. They may not eat when fed. They may shred the couch. Ruin the rug. Tear the drape. But, unlike humans, they do not wound. Instead they awe" (Stephen J. O'Brien, "The Human/Cat Connection," *National Geographic* 191, no. 6 [June 1997]: pp. 77–79). Dogs, on the other hand, eat everything in sight. They shred the entire room simply by walking across it. They ruin your pristine white duvet cover just by settling in for a long, afternoon nap. They tear the cabinet door off its hinges to get to yesterday's trash. And, like humans, they wound to the core. Just take a trip to the store without hoisting Otis into the front seat, and imagine what those dopey, sad, pitiful eyes are saying as you speed away.

For most of us, dogs and cats play a central role in our everyday lives. We depend upon them for unconditional love, companionship, friendship, and a bit of emotional sustenance. We love them and hate them. We spend more money at the vets than we do on our own skin rashes and wayward teeth. We buy toys and brushes and chrome bowls and pure water and the very best food. We groom them and fluff them and stroke them ever so many more times than we do friends or family members. And, as teachers, we have found the pure magic dogs and cats create as learning tools in a classroom. Children, like the elderly, are drawn to them. They light up when any kind of story has a dog and cat as a central figure.

This chapter puts dogs and cats in the center ring for learning. And, with this particular chapter, there will be many children's books, some old, some new, to use as incentives for understanding more about these particular animals and to engage students in a clearer understanding of certain concepts and skills that can be gained by using cats and dogs as a focus.

So, let's get this chapter off to a rousing and cat-centered beginning with a children's book that has been around for a while. *What the Cat Saw* by Ashley Wolff (New York: Walker and Company, 1985). This book has a great repetitive line running through it and makes for an excellent sequencing activity for children. All you need are about 100 pictures of *your* cat. I know you say, that's easier said than done. Not really! If you love your cat, you'll have a camera available at all times when little Fluffy does the most adorable things, like sleeping in the sock drawer, on the computer, on the table, during dinner, in the sink, on your pillow, in the bookcase next to your Walt Whitman first edition, or anywhere else it finds to take over.

Now back to the idea. Take the 100 photos of your cat, spread them all over the floor, then read Wolff's book to the kids. When you are finished, have students get in groups of five, select 8–10 photos, depending on age, put the 8–10 pictures in sequential order, create a story to go along with the ordered photos, and end the story with the line, "... and that is what the cat saw." You've just created a state standard lesson on sequencing and creative writing, and the children have had a delicious time connecting with something they love . . . cats.

I'm looking at my two cats, Boo and Thugg, who, at this moment, are sitting squarely on my computer keys as I try to write this, and my sense is that there wouldn't be quite the impact if you did this same activity with, say, a gerbil, a parakeet, or a goldfish.

You go to Lake Tahoe with a group of women friends for the sole purpose of rediscovering yourself and your dreams upon reaching the interesting and somewhat scary age of 50. You find it harder than you thought. So you delve into tarot cards, full body massages, numerology, the I-ching, and anything else that may hold a clue to what these 50+ years were all about. You take long walks around the lake with these friends and let important discussions lead you through the days. And when the analyses are all in, you find that you are too complacent and balanced. You immediately read this to mean that you need a dog.

So you get on the plane in Reno, fly back to Arizona, look in the paper under "Pets," and search for the right one. Papillon? No, too French. Schnauzer? No, too small. Rottweiler? No, too scary. Poodle? No, too, well, just too.

Then you spot it. The perfect choice. So you get in your car, drive to Phoenix, where it is 114 degrees, walk to the door of the breeder's house, go to the back, sit in the grass, and wait for her to let the puppies out. And out they come, frolicking, licking, jumping, twirling toward you. One of them looks you square in the eyes, and you know.

You name him immediately, bundle him into your shaking arms, put him in the car, turn on a Carlos Nakai CD, and you and Bubba, the wondrous eight-week-old Old English sheepdog, head for home and a new adventure.

And in an instant, you have the makings of a brilliant lesson on dogs. A teachable moment has snuggled itself into your life, and you are ever so pleased.

Activity 1

Content: Math

Lesson: Logic, Drawing Conclusions

Standards: Students will draw inductive and deductive conclusions. Students will interpret statements made with precise language of logic.

Multiple Intelligences: Verbal/Linguistic: Students will listen to a story being read and interpret that story. Logical/Mathematical and Visual/Spatial: Students will draw, label, and/or construct an object.

Materials: Art paper, pens, crayons, small cardboard boxes

Grade Level: 3

Objective: Students will read or listen to a story, then draw or construct an object that will solve a problem found in the story.

Before: Ask students to bring pictures of their dogs to class. Classify them according to "weirdness."

First: Read *Dog Eared* by Amanda Harvey (New York: Doubleday Books for Young Readers, 2002). Have a verbal discussion with the children on the best way to fix Otis's big ears. Write suggestions on the board.

Next: Students, in pairs, will draw a device or invention that will solve the problem of Otis's big ears. Students will label the different aspects of the new invention.

Then: Students will share the devices and/or drawings and come to conclusions on why the devices might work or why they won't.

Finally: Students will share personal stories of the physical idiosyncrasies of their own animals. They may share ways those idiosyncrasies can be fixed.

Alternative Assessment: Write or tell a success story about Otis and his new ears.

Activity 2

Content: Language Arts

Lesson: Children's Literature and Creative Writing

Standard: Students will write a personal narrative or creative story.

Multiple Intelligences: Verbal/Linguistic: Students will read a book and write a story. Visual/Spatial: Students will draw appropriate clothes for an appropriate object. Logical/Mathematical: Students will problem solve to find reasons why animals don't wear clothing.

Materials: Specified children's book

Grade Level: 2–3

Objective: Students will listen to and read a children's book. Students will create a picture from the book's information and write a creative story about the character(s) in the book.

Before: Put the names of a few animals on the board (dog, cat, pig, horse, sheep, snake, gerbil). Lead a discussion on why these animals should not wear clothing. Make a chart of the answers.

First: Read *Cinderella* by William Wegman with Carole Kismaric and Marvin Heiferman (New York: Hyperion, 1993). Students will select three pictures from the book. The teacher will make photocopies of these pictures. Students will cut out the pictures of the photocopied dogs and create paper doll clothes to cover the dogs.

Next: Students will draw a scene in which to place the three newly clothed dogs.

Then: Students will write an original story to accompany the newly clothed dogs.

Finally: Students will share stories, and then create a community bulletin board of the newly attired animals. This bulletin board may be used as a writing stimulus on a periodic basis. Students will share personal stories regarding ways in which their own animals were dressed up for specific occasions, such as Halloween or birthday parties.

Alternative Assessment: Read Judi and Ron Barrett's classic, *Animals Should Definitely Not Wear Clothing* (New York: Atheneum Publishing Company, 1971). Create a discussion with the children about the pitfalls their newly attired dogs might face if they, indeed, wore these types of clothing.

Activity 3

Content: Science, Language Arts

Lesson: Behavior in Dogs

Standard: Students will identify characteristics of animals that allow them to live in specific environments. Students will describe relationships in familial systems. Students will use the writing process to complete a report.

Multiple Intelligences: Interpersonal: Students will give reports and teach others what they know. Visual/Spatial: Students will illustrate their reports on dog behaviors.

Materials: Computer, art paper

Grade Level: 3

Objective: Students will read a children's book and use that book as a stimulus to research behavior in dogs.

Before: Put the following list of behavioral characteristics of dogs on the board: friendly dogs, protective dogs, independent dogs, self-assured dogs, consistent dogs, steady dogs, clever dogs. Discuss the definitions of "friendly," "protective," "independent," "self-assured," and so on.

First: Read *Chewy Louie* by Howie Scheider (Flagstaff, AZ: Rising Moon, 2000).

Next: Students will use the Internet to research various breeds that exhibit particular behavioral characteristics.

Then: Students will select one characteristic and one breed to use as a basis for a report to the class. Students will illustrate their selected breed in addition to giving the report.

Finally: Through writing, speaking, or drawing, students will conclude which characteristics best fit their own pets.

Alternative Assessment: Use the collected reports and illustrations to create a class booklet and to teach kindergartners all about dog behaviors.

Activity 4

Content: Math

Lesson: Problem Solving with Original Animal Heroes/Heroines

Standards: Students will predict the likelihood of events. Students will draw inductive and deductive conclusions.

Multiple Intelligences: Visual/Spatial: Students will draw a dog hero. Verbal/Linguistic: Students will discuss and share stories about dog heroes.

Materials: Art paper, crayons

Grade Level: 2–3

Objective: Students will draw an original comic dog hero (e.g., spider dog, super dog, and so on). Students will create a community bulletin board of these characters and use it as a stimulus for problem solving.

Before: Create a discussion around personal acts of heroism among animals and among dogs in particular.

First: Read *Dogzilla* by Dav Pilkey (Boston: Harcourt, Brace and Company, 2002).

Next: Students will draw an original comic dog hero and label all the aspects that make the dog a hero. Students will discuss, by viewing each other's work, what makes a hero.

Then: Students will discuss heroes in their own lives and the similar characteristics of the personal heroes.

Finally: Students will write a journal entry entitled, "I was a hero once when I _____."

Alternative Assessment: Once a week, students will share hero stories and review characteristics that were demonstrated. Students will use the community board of dog heroes as a stimulus for comparisons.

Activity 5

Content: Language Arts, Math

Lesson: Writing a Story, Sequencing

Standards: Students will use the writing process to complete a variety of writing tasks. Students will write a creative story.

Multiple Intelligences: Verbal/Linguistic: Students will write a story. Visual/Spatial: Students will use illustrations from a book as a guide for writing. Logical/Mathematical: Students will answer problem-solving questions.

Materials: None

Grade Level: 3

Objective: Students will look at a wordless picture book and use the illustrations as a guide for writing a story that accompanies the illustrations.

Before: Show the wordless picture book, *A Day, a Dog* by Gabrielle Vincent (Asheville, NC: Front Street, 1999). Discuss the illustrations. Make predictions. Looking at the illustrations, use the beginning phrase "I wonder" to stimulate interest. Suggested "I wonder" questions may include:

> *I wonder* why the owner threw the dog out of the car?
>
> *I wonder* what the dog thought as he was thrown out?
>
> *I wonder* what kind of conversation the people in the car had after the dog was thrown from the car?
>
> *I wonder* how the dog kept from being hit by other cars?
>
> *I wonder* how the people showed their anger when the dog caused them to wreck their cars?
>
> *I wonder* how dogs feel or show fear?
>
> *I wonder* what nights alone felt like to the dog?
>
> *I wonder* how the dog found food?
>
> *I wonder* how the dog kept going?
>
> *I wonder* why the young boy was alone?
>
> *I wonder* how I would end the story?

First: Using the class discussions as a guide, on the board write the sequence of events that occur in the story. Pay particular attention to how students choose to end the story.

Next: Students will use that sequence of events to assist them in the retelling and rewriting of the story in their own words.

Then: Students will read the stories to each other.

Finally: Students will reflect upon the treatment of animals in general through discussion, artwork, or journal entries, such as "If I were to find a stray dog, I'd _____."

Alternative Assessment: Take a field trip to the local animal shelter. Students will interview workers there and ask questions relating to the humane treatment of animals.

Activity 6

Content: Language Arts

Lesson: Point of View

Standard: Students will write a report that conveys a point of view.

Multiple Intelligences: Verbal/Linguistic: Students will write a caption or report. Visual/Spatial: Students will use photography as a stimulus for gathering information.

Materials: None

Grade Level: 2–3

Objective: Students will look at a book on cats and write point of view captions to go with pictures in the book. Students will use certain photos to tell an add-on story.

Before: Show pictures in the book *Funny Cats* by Jane Martin, edited by J.C. Suares (New York: Stewart, Tabori & Chang, 1995).

First: Show the photograph on page 5 of the above book. Ask the class to discuss *to whom* the cat is writing, and what the topic of the letter might be.

Next: The students will select three photos from the book and write point of view captions for the photos.

Then: Students, in groups of five, will choose one photo and create a verbal add-on story simply by looking at the picture as they speak.

Finally: Students will share one true fact about the life of a cat.

Alternative Assessment: Students will draw an illustration showing three true facts about cats.

Activity 7

Content: Science

Lesson: Comparing Characteristics in the Cat Family

Standards: Students will identify characteristics of plants and animals that allow them to live in specific environments. Students will locate and use resources to write an informational report.

Multiple Intelligences: Verbal/Linguistic: Students will use research skills to gather information about certain cat lineages. Visual/Spatial: Students will create a visual representation of the survival characteristic information. Logical/Mathematical: Students will create a comparison chart of combined information gathered from the various research reports.

Materials: Art supplies

Grade Level: 3

Objective: Students, in pairs or groups of three, will research one member of the cat family and compare the different characteristics used for surviving in specific environments.

Before: Using *National Geographic* 191, no. 6 (June 1997) as a basis for resource as well as the Internet, students will gather information from the family of cats found in this particular issue. Lineages for study include domestic cats, pumas (cheetah, jaguarundi), ocelots, and panthers (lion, tiger, jaguar, leopard).

First: Students will write a report based on the survival characteristics of the particular member of the cat family that was selected for the report.

Next: Students will use a visual medium (drawings, clay art, diorama, mobile, "found objects art," water colors, and so on) to represent the research findings in a visual way.

Then: Students will present the reports to each other and create a comparison chart on chart paper as the reports are given.

Finally: Students will create an open discussion of various ways their own domesticated cats survive in their different home environments. Students will write a journal entry entitled, "Surviving in the Wilderness."

Alternative Assessment: Use the information gathered from the comparison chart. Create cards with questions on them. Students will play a form of Pictionary as a form of review.

Activity 8

Content: Language Arts

Lesson: Reinforcing Phonetic Skills through Lyric Writing

Standards: Students will use phonetic skills to decode words. Students will use word recognition and decoding strategies to comprehend written selections. Students will interpret visual clues that enhance the comprehension of texts.

Multiple Intelligence: Musical/Rhythmic: Students will sing a song about cats.

Materials: Copy of lyrics, chart paper

Grade Level: 2–3

Objective: Students will sing a song and use the lyrics to reinforce appropriate phonetic skills.

Before: Put the following song, "A Little Kitty," on chart paper.

A Little Kitty

(Tune: "Makin' Whoopee" from the children's CD *Purple Dinosaur*)

A dash of red, a dot of white,
a splash of black, as thick as night.
It's not the weather,
it's something better.
A little kitty.
A baby nose that's pink as dawn,
a mouth that shows a lazy yawn.
It's not your sister,
but let me whisper
that it's a kitty.
Picture a perfect fur ball
sprinkled with lots of sun.
Lean close and hear it purring

Bowling's not this much fun.
It sometimes hides, but then on cue
it starts to meow its vowels for you.
It's not your mother, or older brother.
It's just a kitty.
(Ten-bar instrumental)
Its nails are long and cause an ouch.
Its fine hair covers the brand new couch.
It crawls up curtains, of that you're certain,
the little kitty.
When it is dark and time for bed,
you grab your pillow, of course, instead
what you are fluffing isn't feather stuffing,
it's just a kitty.
When you are deep in slumber
dreaming of that special place.
Kitty is wildly running
first up, then down your face.

So what's the answer, what do you do?
Go get another. Then you'll have two.
Life will be sweeter. Don't dwell on litter.
Just love your kitties.
Just love your kitties.
Just love your kitties
Love on your kitties.
Play with your kitties.

(Music by Gus Kahn, 1928 Lyrics by Martha Brady, 1999)

First: Gather a large selection of cat pictures. Students will sing the song, then try to find pictures of cats that depict different aspects of the song such as colors of cats, facial expressions, actions, physical appearances, and so on.

Next: Use the lyrics to this kitty song to reinforce the following comprehension strategies, phonetic skills, word recognitions, literary elements, or correct conventions:

1. Nouns and pronouns
2. Contractions
3. Verbs
4. Adjectives
5. Punctuation
6. Word decoding
7. Literary elements
8. Others

Then: Students will use creative expression to write their own lyrics to the song. Using the following format, students will fill in the blanks with their own appropriate words.

A Little Kitty

A dash of _____, a dot of _____
a splash of _____, as thick as night.
It's not the weather
it's something better,
a little kitty.
A baby nose that's pink as _____.
A mouth that shows a lazy _____.
It's not your sister
but let me whisper
that it's a kitty.
Picture a perfect fur ball
sprinkled with lots of _____.
Lean close and hear it purring.
_____'s not this much fun.
It sometimes hides, but then on cue
It starts to meow and _____ for you.
It's not your mother, or older brother
It's just a kitty.
(*Ten-bar instrumental*)
Its nails are long and cause an _____.
Its fine hair covers the brand new _____.
It crawls up curtains, of that you're certain,
the little kitty.
When it is dark and time for _____,
You grab your pillow, of course, instead
What you are fluffing isn't feather stuffing
It's just a kitty.
When you are deep in slumber
Dreaming of that special _____.
Kitty is wildly running
First up, then down your _____.
So what's the answer, what do you do?
Go get another. Then you'll have _____.
Life will be _____. Don't dwell on litter.
Just love your kitties.
Just love your kitties.
Just _____ your kitties
Love on your kitties.
_____ with your kitties.

Finally: Students will look at the pictures of the cats one more time. Using these pictures as a basis, they will write a personal story of one adventure they have had with their pet cats.

Alternative Assessment: Students will use research found when writing about nondomesticated cats (lions, tigers, pumas, leopards, and so on) and write their own lyrics about one type of wildcat.

Activity 9

Content: Language Arts

Lesson: Myths

Standard: Students will write a personal narrative or creative story.

Multiple Intelligences: Bodily/Kinesthetic: Students will act out myths. Verbal/Linguistics: Students will write myths.

Materials: None

Grade Level: 3

Objective: Students will write a personal myth about one characteristic of a cat.

Before: Read the children's book *I Am the Cat* by Alice Schertle, illustrations by Mark Buehner (New York: Lothrop, Lee and Shepard Books, 1999). Make distinctions between the catlike actions stated in the book and the myths that describe those actions.

First: Discuss actions, such as the following, that come to mind when describing the behavior of cats: licking paws, having nine lives, walking quietly, meowing, drinking milk, prowling at night, arching the back, coughing up hairballs, and so on.

Next: Students will choose an action and write a short myth that describes how the action came to be.

Then: Students will act out their actions and their myths, either verbally or nonverbally.

Finally: Students will think of a personal idiosyncratic action they have and think about a myth that may answer why they do it.

Alternative Assessment: Read an actual myth. Compare it to some of the myths found in this children's book.

Activity 10

Content: Social Studies

Lesson: Places in the World

Standard: Students will identify natural characteristics of places and how people and animals interact with their environment.

Multiple Intelligence: Bodily/Kinesthetic: Students will use maps and globes.

Materials: Globe, world map

Grade Level: 3

Objective: Students will research, through map study and resources, several natural places in the world. Students will use this information and a selected children's book to write ending statements that are appropriate to these locations.

Before: Read *When Martha's Away* by Bruce Ingman (Boston: Houghton Mifflin Company, 1995).

First: Use a globe or world map to isolate ten or so areas such as a specific desert, ocean, country, city, jungle, river, mountain, and so on. Discuss the physical characteristics of each site using the following guidelines:

    a. Climate

    b. Peculiarity

    c. Physical makeup

    d. Relationship to people

Next: Students will choose one physical place in the world. Using the theme of the book *When Martha's Away* and the information about the specific place, they will complete this phrase, "When (student's name) away in (the specific location, such as desert), (pet cat's name) will _____." The end of this phrase must use appropriate reasoning of what a cat might actually do if in one of these locales.

Then: Phrases will be shared in class, and a Q & A session will take place in order to ensure that answers are authentic and have been researched appropriately.

Finally: Students will think of things their own cats might be doing while they are in school.

Alternative Assessment: None

✔ *And now, what about five good lessons from one good book?* See if these work.

The book: Alderton, David. Illustrated by Trevor Dunton. (1998). *My Cat: Pet Photo Album.* London: Marshall Editions Ltd.

1. Students will keep a daily journal about the happenings, tricks, misdemeanors, and otherwise daily routines of their cats.
2. Students will teach a lesson on one aspect of taking care of a cat.
3. Students will take photos of their cats and create their own cat photo albums.
4. Students will look online to research 3–5 different breeds of cats. Once the facts have been gathered, students will create fact mobiles displaying what they have learned.
5. Students will interview a veterinarian about preventative health issues relating to cats.

✔ *Oh yes. Remember the teachable moment* that introduced our activities in this chapter? Well, here is a little lesson to go with that idea.

Activity 11

Content: Writing

Lesson: Using Newspaper Ads as a Stimulus for Writing

Standards: Students will gather, organize, and report information. Students will use the writing process to write a newspaper ad.

Multiple Intelligence: Verbal/Linguistic: Students will read for information. Students will engage in a writing activity.

Materials: Pet section of the newspaper

Grade Level: 3

Objective: Students will gather information from a newspaper source and write an original ad.

Before: Here we go with the digital camera again. This time, take the camera to a local pet store and shoot pictures of several puppies of varying breeds. Jot down information regarding each puppy such as cost, age, breed, and so on.

First: Bring the pictures back and lead the students in a discussion of how much each puppy might cost and how old each puppy might be in the picture. Students will generate discussions about how to describe each puppy to a person who cannot see the pictures.

Next: In groups, students will look at the "Pets" section of the newspaper. They will be looking for descriptors, cost, age, and general information placed in the newspaper as a means of describing the puppies to potential buyers. Teacher will put the 5 W's on the board (who, what, when, where, and why) and give a brief lesson on how those are used when writing newspaper ads.

Then: In groups, students will select one of the pet store puppy pictures and the facts gathered from the newspapers, then write their own newspaper advertisements.

Finally: Students will take the completed writing task and pictures to the computer lab, where the pictures will be scanned and the writing piece will be rewritten on the computer. Completed work will be collated into a booklet.

Alternative Assessment: Students will use the school as a research area for locating puppies or kittens that are being given away or sold. Students will use the same sequence of events to create real-life ads for those animals. These newly written ads will be placed on a bulletin board in the school office for all to see.

And finally, if you think *a picture is worth a thousand words,* use the *Cats and Dogs* drawing on the next page to engage your students in seeing, writing, drawing, or just thinking about the wonderful creatures who seem to consume our hearts and daily lives. The following activities will work wonders for boys and girls who love animals and who will benefit more if they can see these cats and dogs through color, shape, form, and design.

Activity 12

Content: Math

Lesson: Prediction, Drawing Conclusions

Standards: Students will predict the likelihood of events. Students will draw inductive and deductive conclusions.

Multiple Intelligences: Logical/Mathematical: Students will problem solve. Visual/Spatial: Students will use shape and form as catalysts for making decisions.

Materials: Copies of the cats and dogs drawing

Grade Level: 1–3

Objective: Students will answer prediction and conclusion questions relating to the cats and dogs drawing.

Before: Lead students in a general discussion of the most unbelievable story they know or have heard about their own dog or cat, or about dogs or cats belonging to other family members or friends.

First: Show the cats and dogs drawing found in this chapter. Lead a discussion whereby students describe and name the animals found in the story. Remind students that the sheepdog already has a name: Bubba.

Next: Ask the following prediction and conclusion questions, using the cats and dogs drawing as a stimulus.

1. "Tell me what these animals will land on to keep them from being hurt."
2. "How did the animals get into the clouds?"
3. "Tell me what would happen if a big gust of wind came and carried these animals even higher in the sky."
4. "Why can't these animals simply stay in the sky or on a cloud?"
5. "What will happen to them when they land?"
6. "What animal do you think will fall to the ground quicker?"
7. "If this were a real story, how would it end?"
8. "If this were an imagined story, how might it end?"
9. "Why do you think none of the animals looked frightened?"
10. "Why is this drawing not a true drawing?"

Then: Students will make up their own prediction or conclusion questions to ask the rest of the class.

Finally: Students will reflect upon the phrase "raining cats and dogs." They will ask family members to define that phrase for them.

Alternative Assessment: Students will share the definitions of the phrase "raining cats and dogs" with each other.

Activity 13

Content: Language Arts, Art

Lesson: Problem Solving through Drawing

Standards: Students will use drawing to express ideas. Students will interpret visual clues that enhance the comprehension of a story.

Multiple Intelligences: Visual/Spatial: Students will draw. Verbal/Linguistic: Students will write.

Materials: Crayons

Grade Level: K–3

Objective: Students will make additional drawings to the cats and dogs drawing and tell a story that comes from the enhanced drawing.

Before: Students will look at the cats and dogs drawing and give it their own titles.

First: Students will draw additional items, objects, people, and so on onto the existing cats and dogs drawing.

Next: Students will tell a story that comes from the newly created drawing.

Then: Students will add one more object to the drawing, one that doesn't quite fit into the whole "sense" of the new drawing.

Finally: Students will reflect upon ways the story changed with the addition of the last object drawn into the picture. Students will retitle the drawing.

Alternative Assessment: Students will journal about why dogs and cats can't fly.

Activity 14

Content: Language Arts

Lesson: Writing a Story

Standards: Students will use effective vocabulary to relate information. Students will write a creative story. Students will use comprehension strategies.

Multiple Intelligences: Verbal/Linguistic: Students will write a story. Visual/Spatial: Students will use visual art as a catalyst for writing.

Materials: Copies of cats and dogs drawing, writing sheets

Grade Level: 2–3

Objective: Students will add descriptive words, action words, and other words to an existing story about the cats and dogs drawing.

Before: Review descriptive and action words.

First: Distribute the following story attached to the cats and dogs drawing.

> Once upon a time there lived _____ cats and two _____. They loved to do tricks. They would climb a tall mountain and _____ onto fluffy _____ that were floating in the blue _____. And when the time was right, the cats and two_____ would jump off the _____ and _____ to the ground. Bubba, a dog, used his fluffy _____ to help him float downward. _____, another dog, used his paws to help him _____ to Earth. The striped _____ used his pointed _____ to hold onto the wind as he fell. The spotted kitty _____ onto the cloud until he fell straight _____. One cat turned over and over in the _____ and fell on his _____. And the kitty with no _____ fell on his bottom when he hit the _____. But no one got hurt because when they all landed on the ground, the big dog landed on a _____, the striped cat landed on a _____, the upside-down cat landed on a _____, the two spotted _____ landed on _____, and the dog with the ring around his _____ landed on a _____. What fun they all had. And since they never got _____, they did this trick over and over and _____.

Next: Students will fill in the blanks and practice reading the completed story to themselves or a partner. Volunteers will read their stories to the rest of the class.

Then: Lead a discussion on the differences between fact and fiction. Students will discuss ways to make their stories more factual than fictitious.

Finally: Students will reflect upon this question, "This story was not believable to me because _____."

Alternative Assessment: Make a list of descriptive or action words that come to mind simply by looking at the cats and dogs drawing.

Activity 15

Content: Arts

Lesson: Re-creating a Drawing

Standard: Students will expand their knowledge and use of different art media.

Multiple Intelligences: Visual/Spatial: Students will draw representations. Bodily/Kinesthetic: Students will construct representations.

Materials: Art supplies

Grade Level: 3

Objective: Students will use other arts media to re-create the cats and dogs drawing.

Before: Set up the room into four arts centers. Center #1 will include modeling clay and construction paper. Center #2 will include watercolors, brushes, and white art paper. Center #3 will include various colors of tissue paper, liquid starch, and construction paper. Center #4 will include socks, stuffing, craft eyes, flannel squares, and so on.

First: Lead the students in a discussion about expressing ideas through art. Show various illustrations and examples of dogs and cats and how various artists represent them.

Next: Give directions about the use of the four arts centers.

Then: Students will choose one of the media centers in which to re-create the cats and dogs drawing. The choices include:

1. Re-creating the drawing through three-dimensional modeling clay replicas placed on construction paper.
2. Re-creating the drawing with watercolors on art paper.
3. Re-creating the drawing with tissue paper, liquid starch, and construction paper.
4. Re-creating one of the animals in the drawing by making a sock puppet.

Finally: Students will reflect upon and compare their work to the cats and dogs drawing.

Alternative Assessment: Students will exhibit their original re-creations of the drawing and tell a visiting class about the process involved.

Activity 16

Content: Language Arts

Lesson: Telling Stories

Standard: Students will use effective vocabulary and organization to relate information.

Multiple Intelligences: Visual/Spatial: Students will use the cats and dogs drawing as a stimulus for telling a story. Verbal/Linguistic: Students will tell a story. Intrapersonal: Students will reflect upon past experiences.

Materials: Copies of the cats and dogs drawing

Grade Level: K–3

Objective: Students will look at the different elements of the drawing in this chapter and tell an original story.

Before: Students will review important aspects of telling a story.

First: Students will use the cats and dogs drawing as a stimulus for telling stories about different experiences happening in the scenes in the picture.

Next: Students will relate personal stories that correspond to the original stories being told.

Then: Students will answer "What would happen if..." questions about the picture.

Finally: Students will reflect upon their own appreciation of the drawing.

Alternative Assessment: Students will take a drawing home and ask a family member to tell them a story that comes from viewing the drawing.

To wrap up this chapter, here is every idea you ever wanted to know about cats and dogs. Give these waggily tail ideas over to your students and see what happens.

Cats and Dogs K–3

V/L Read, tell, and compare cat or dog stories.	Give reports about cats and their places in cultures.	Create poems from cat or dog pictures or photos.	Discuss illustrators' perceptions of dogs.	Write celebrities or local politicians about their pets.
L/M Chart collective information from students' pets.	Create a personal timeline of your pet.	Compare certain human traits to animal traits.	Study a can of cat food from production to consumption.	Use cat or dog photos to make predictions.
V/S Design and label the "perfect dog house" in three different countries.	Create a collage of dog or cat faces from magazines.	Use clay to create the perfect dog to go into the perfect houses.	Draw and design an original can of dog or cat food.	Create an illustrative ABC book about dogs or cats.
B/K Create peep-box habitats of cats in the wild.	Videotape the interviews.	Create an audio library of favorite dog or cat stories.	Make and bake "dog bones" in class.	Take a field trip to a pet store.
M/R Teach "Old McDonald" with new lyrics that are solely about cats and dogs.	Create sound effects to accompany the reading of pet stories.	Clap the musical patterns of this song.	Create a call/response rhythm focusing on cats and dogs.	Create hand jives for certain species of wild cats.
Inter Teach the class a trick that has been taught a pet.	Interview cat or dog owners.	Present information to the class.	"Pitch" a commercial for the new can of cat or dog food.	Teach a map skill lesson about the three countries.
Intra Reflect upon how you would keep a pet healthy.	Draw an ideal pet for your particular family.	"If your pet could talk, what would be its first sentence?"	"It would be good to have a dog in the classroom because _____."	"Cats might not work in the classroom because _____."
N Discuss habitat and survival connections.	Research one well-known zoo.	Observe puppies and kitties in action.	Trace the life cycle of your cat or dog.	Create a list of specific questions to ask pet store owners.

The activities and experiences in this grid are just a bit more difficult and can bring some challenges to your students. These ideas can be used as extension lessons or individual projects, or, in some cases, in learning centers.

Cats and Dogs 4–6

V/L	Find a book that best describes your own cat or dog.	Research cats and the Egyptian culture.	Discuss responses to the words and music.	Write a myth about a cat or dog.	Use illustrator's drawings to write original texts.
L/M	Write math story problems about your pets.	Create a genealogy of a certain ancient breed of dog.	Draw inductive and deductive conclusions about these.	Compare ingredients in three types of dog food.	Use math techniques to facilitate these computations.
V/S	Design a dog or cat as a machine. Label the parts and their functions.	Look at works of art that focus on dogs or cats.	Draw one of these works of art in your own style.	Create a brochure for a new dog or cat food.	Illustrate myths and create a community myth book.
B/K	Create peep-box scenes from these findings.	Videotape interviews with teachers about their pets.	Create an audio library of factual information regarding cats and dogs.	Create an agility course for stuffed dogs or cats.	Take a trip to a local zoo.
M/R	Listen to Andrew Lloyd Webber's soundtrack of *Cats.*	Use the melody from one of the songs to write lyrics about any cat, wild or domestic.	Sing the song, "A Little Kitty." Focus on hearing the melody, then following that melody in tune.	Sing songs from other cultures that relate to cats or dogs.	Using one of the animals in the children's books in this chapter, write and perform a rap.
Inter	Teach about your pet and its connection to this book.	Interview school personnel about their own dogs or cats. Ask the same questions to each interviewee.	In groups, "pitch" ad campaign ideas about this new dog food.	Teach one of these songs from another culture to the class.	Lead a debate about using dogs for research.
Intra	Lead a general discussion on the importance of dogs or cats in your own home.	What have you learned from your dog or cat?	How do your personal life qualities compare with your dog's or cat's?	"The classroom would be a calmer place if dogs were allowed because _____."	"Cats know more than I do because _____."
N	Discuss physical characteristics that assist big cats living in the wild.	Keep an exercise log on yourself and one on your dog.	Observe behavioral characteristics in the big cats.	Use the Internet to gather scientific information regarding this topic.	Research, then ask cause-and-effect questions regarding the big cats.

DWELLINGS

Dear Teacher,

When we want children to learn about people of other cultures and about themselves as well, we must not forget to include, in an important way, the study of where people live and the structures in which they dwell, especially the differences in those structures and what they provide for survival, adaptability, and custom. We want children to know why igloos work best in some areas, and why thatched-roofed round houses work best in other environments, and why both of those abodes have an important connection to the custom, ritual, and behavior of the people who dwell there.

Central to these issues, we wish for children to know about their own homes and how they, too, differ from each other's homes and the homes of children around the world.

That said, let us take a field trip in our mind. Ask the children to close their eyes and try to visualize the first thing that comes to mind about the houses in which they live. Do they see the front door, the backyard, their bedroom, and the kitchen? Do they envision the sofa, the TV, the garage where their bikes are stored? Lead a discussion on the things or spaces they deem important in their own homes. Ask them questions about their homes, such as:

1. Where are you the safest in your house? Why?

2. What is your favorite room? Why?

3. If you could change your home, how would you change it?

4. Describe the outside of your home.

5. If you invited a friend over, what is the first thing you would show that friend about your house?

6. Describe your own room.

7. Pretend your home was accidentally placed in the (desert) (jungle) (swamp) (Arctic). How would living in your home be different in those environments?

8. Close your eyes. On a piece of paper, draw the front of your house by memory.

9. With a partner, describe in detail what your backyard looks like.

10. Describe your house in five words.

To begin this chapter on dwellings, which also includes a few activities focusing on animal habitats, give students each a piece of white art paper and access to many magazines. Students will cut out pictures from the magazines and re-create either the interior of their houses or simply their bedrooms. Once these "blueprints" are completed, use these re-creations as stimuli for writing. Some suggested writing and/or discussion activities and titles may include:

1. What Is under My Bed?
2. I Hear a Noise
3. Where Is My Puppy?
4. Who Is at the Front Door?
5. The Lost Toy
6. Getting Ready for School
7. Here Kitty, Kitty
8. Sounds in the Dark
9. Patterns
10. Hidden Things

Once you have stimulated the children's interests about their own homes, it is time to branch out to other dwellings or habitats. There are so many good websites that can complement your lessons on these topics. Two of my favorites at the moment give good, solid information on backyard habitats and castles, two dwelling topics in which most children are very interested. www.nwf.org/backyardwildlifehabitat/ is a National Wildlife Federation site that is full of kid-friendly information that can embellish any habitat lesson. Beginning with what children know in their own environment creates authentic lessons right off the bat and gives students a built-in backyard lab to pursue the whole idea of habitats that they can see and study on a daily basis. Surfnetkids.com is filled with a myriad of teachable ideas, one of which is castles, a real student turn-on. At this site there is information about castles found in other countries and, more importantly, castles found in the United States and perhaps in your own state as well. Both of these sites are good places to begin an online adventure with kids about these places that all of us, somewhere in the world or even in our own backyard, call home.

One evening when you are feeling overly nostalgic and a wee bit old, you begin to think about the house in which you were born and spent part of your childhood. The memories flow by and you begin to remember the important events that occurred in that house. Soon the stories come at such a fast pace that you realize you need places to catch them, so your mind takes you to the other houses you called home. One by one these dwellings begin to stand, side by side, in your past, and like a familiar neighborhood, the moment takes you from one house to the other, carving out events and etching them into your present. You stop and think of the different memories these houses provided, and you realize that children have memories too.

You look at the stream of houses that filter into your mind's eye, and each house dangles like newly washed sheets on your mother's clothesline. And in an instant you have the makings of a brilliant lesson on homes. A teachable moment has constructed itself into your life, and you are ever so pleased.

Activity 1

Content: Math

Lesson: Measurement

Standard: Students will understand and demonstrate the concept of measurement.

Multiple Intelligences: Logical/Mathematical: Students will create a space to scale. Students will estimate cost and amount. Verbal/Linguistic: Students will listen to a story and discuss its meaning.

Materials: None

Grade Level: 3+

Objective: The students will read a children's book and use mathematical, estimation, and measurement skills to recreate a structure from the book.

Before: Students will estimate the length and width of the classroom. They will use measuring tape and/or rulers to accurately measure the room's size.

First: Using that information, students will measure a perimeter in the room that is ten feet long and fifteen feet wide. Students will define that perimeter with string, rope, or chairs. Students will sit on the floor in that defined space.

Next: Read *Henry Builds a Cabin* by D.B. Johnson (Boston: Houghton Mifflin Company, 2002).

Then: Students will use different math skills to estimate the amount of the following materials needed to build a cabin 10' × 15'.

1. Pieces of lumber
2. Packets of shingles
3. Windows
4. Bricks
5. Nails
6. Hinges and screws
7. Latches
8. Doors

As a follow-up to these mathematical efforts, students may take a field trip to Home Depot or any hardware store and interview and ask questions of persons who can help estimate or figure out this information.

Finally: Students will discuss pros and cons of living in a space that size. Such leading questions may include:

1. How would living in this small space change your life?
2. What would you have to give up?
3. Where would people sleep?
4. How would you use the outside as part of your house?

5. How would living in a space this size be different than where you live now?

6. What would be positive about living in a space this size?

7. Research one-room cabins or houses on the Internet. Share the information with each other.

8. Why do people "need" so much room in which to live?

9. Where is wasted space in your own home?

10. In what areas in your own home do you spend the most time?

Alternative Assessment: Give a biography report on Henry David Thoreau, or write descriptively about the part of your house that is your favorite space.

Activity 2

Content: Science

Lesson: Nests

Standard: Students will construct models that illustrate simple concepts and compare them to what they represent.

Multiple Intelligences: Bodily/Kinesthetic: Students will construct birds' nests. Verbal/ Linguistics: Students will write, in some form, about birds' nests. Intrapersonal: Students will reflect through journal writing.

Materials: Materials for birds' nests (see below, under "First" section, for examples)

Grade Level: 3

Objective: Students will demonstrate an understanding of how birds' nests are built. Students will use found objects to construct birds' nests and compare those models to appropriate examples.

Before: Using facts and illustrations found in the Dorling-Kindersley (1988) science resource book, *Birds*, students will discuss the differences, similarities, and peculiarities in the construction of specific birds' nests.

First: Students will collect the following materials to create birds' nests in the classroom: seed, twigs, leaves, string, tin foil, twine, torn paper, feathers, moss, grass, hair (from brushes), and mud mixture. Students will use previously gathered facts to bring authenticity into their constructions.

Next: Students will use the completed birds' nests as catalysts for writing experiences, whether they be poetry, factual sheets, fact cards, "Did you know?" questions, and so on.

Then: Students will share the nests and written information with other classrooms before displaying these creations in the library.

Finally: Students will journal with these statements: "Birds feel safe in their nests because_____." and "I wouldn't feel safe in their nests because_____."

Alternative Assessment: Students will play a musical chairs game of facts about birds' nests.

Activity 3

Content: Science

Lesson: Habitats

Standard: Students will identify the characteristics of certain animals that allow them to live in specific environments.

Multiple Intelligences: Visual/Spatial: Students will observe habitats in an environment. Bodily/Kinesthetic: Students will build glass jar habitats. Intrapersonal: Students will reflect upon their personal connection to various habitats.

Materials: Magnifying glasses

Grade Level: 2–3

Objective: Students will take a field trip around the school, observe various habitats available, and create habitats in a jar.

Before: Read Nic Bishop's *Backyard Detective: Critters up Close* (New York: Scholastic, 2002). Students will share stories of personal discoveries of various animal or insect habitats in their own backyards.

First: Students will brainstorm and make a list of places in and around the school where animal or insect habitats may be found. Lead the class to an understanding that such habitats may be found on leaves, flowers, grass, trees, vegetables, or fruit and in other hidden areas inside the school building and out on the playground.

Next: Students will create an "identify and record" sheet to use when on the habitat field trip. A simple sheet may be similar to the following:

Habitat Field Trip

Field Notes

Name _____ Date _____

Animal/Insect _____

Location _____

1. Written Observation (Write a paragraph of what you observe.)

2. Drawing Observation (Draw, in detail, what is observed.)

3. New Discovery (Write a sentence describing one thing that you learned in your observation of this habitat.)

4. Known Fact (Write a sentence describing one thing that you already knew about this habitat.)

Then: Students will use the field notes sheet as a guide as they re-create the observed habitat in a glass jar.

Finally: Students will become teachers for each other as they create a habitat museum and go from jar to jar learning about habitats found in and around the school and playground. Students will also add a reflective component to these shared lessons by comparing the habitats they have chosen to the habitat in which they live. A sample statement may say, "The habitat in which the _____ lives is similar to my own because _____" or "The habitat in which the _____ lives would not work for me because _____."

Alternative Assessment: Students will create a class mural that includes drawings and labeling of the various habitats observed on the class field trip.

Activity 4

Content: Social Studies

Lesson: Houses around the World

Standard: Students will use geographic knowledge to explain and understand the adaptability of structures in certain global areas.

Multiple Intelligence: Visual/Spatial: Students will draw global homes.

Materials: Art paper, drawing pencils or pens

Grade Level: 3

Objective: Students will research various global homes, draw these homes, and compile the drawings into a classroom coloring book.

Before: Students will use white art paper to draw the house in which they live.

First: Students will select and research one of the following types of global homes: sod houses, floating houses, castles, tipis, dugout houses, tree huts, thatched-roofed houses, igloos, yurts, cliff dwellings, and others that come to mind.

Next: Students will use the information from their research to draw a representation of these homes, one home per student. Students will use the same size and type art paper and pen or pencil. Drawings will be placed on the top two thirds of the art paper, leaving an empty space at the bottom for writing activities. One of the writing pieces to be included will be a short fact statement about the selected global home that is depicted in the drawing.

Then: The drawings will be revised and reworked until each student's "best work" is turned in. Drawings will be compiled and placed in a bound booklet. Teacher can direct students to use this booklet in the following ways:

1. Color each global dwelling to their own liking.
2. Write a point of view piece appropriate to each drawing.
3. Write a creative narrative piece for each drawing.

4. Write a poem about the pictures.

5. Add three or more objects to these drawings, and write about how the addition of these objects changed a storyline.

6. Write more facts about each global home.

7. Write reflective pieces about the drawings.

8. Add appropriate background landscaping scenes to each drawing.

9. Place them into a drawing scene and write a story or paragraph.

10. Use all of the drawings to create *if* and *then* scenarios.

Finally: Students will select one drawing and talk about how their own family lives would be different if they lived in that type of global dwelling.

Alternative Assessment: Choosing one of the global drawings and in groups of four, students will present a simple puppet play that depicts a day in the life of a child living in that environment.

Activity 5

Content: Social Studies

Lesson: Traditional Dwelling Board Game

Standard: Students will identify natural and human characteristics of places and how people interact with their environment.

Multiple Intelligence: Bodily/Kinesthetic: Students will play a game.

Materials: Poster board, markers, maps

Grade Level: 3

Objective: Students will create and play a board game to review or learn facts about traditional dwellings.

Before: Divide students into four groups or more. Give each group types of global dwellings, such as igloos, tipis, nomadic tents, and rain forest houses, for which to research facts. Students will find ten facts about each global shelter. These facts will be made into fact cards.

First: Students will create the game board, which may consist of a piece of poster board on which is glued maps of countries or regions in which the selected global shelters can be found. For example, if igloos, tipis, nomadic tents, and rain forest houses are researched, small maps of arctic areas, the plains area of the United States, Middle Eastern countries, and rain forest regions will be glued on the surface of the poster board.

Next: Students will brainstorm ideas of how to begin each game, where to place each move step, and how one person wins the game.

Then: Students in groups will design and construct their own game boards, using one of two formats. One method will have the children focus on one global shelter, for example, igloos. Thus, the game, board, and fact questions will concentrate only on that one type of dwelling. Another method will have the students select four dwellings from four diverse areas. Thus, the game board maps will include all four regions, and the fact cards will include information about the four designated areas.

Finally: Students will create the board games and play each other's games. Here is a suggested board game idea using igloos, tipis, nomadic tents, and rain forest houses as the selected global dwellings.

Directions for 2–4 players

1. Students begin at START and roll die.

   Students choose and answer one card from the card stack.

2. If the correct answer is given, students advance the number of squares equal to the number on the die.

3. If a player lands on an "oops!" space, the player does not draw a card but "sits out" in the closest map area until another player answers a question relating to that particular map area. When a correct answer is given, the player who was "sitting out" goes back to the original space in which the turn was lost.

4. Players continue reading cards, answering them, and advancing their tokens.

5. The first player who lands a token on the END square and correctly answers the question drawn wins.

The following assorted questions can be typed and placed on cards, then shuffled for random selection. Answers can be placed on an answer key sheet.

Igloos

a. When igloos were built for use over a long period of time, what shape igloo worked best?
(round)

b. If igloos are built in a rectangular shape, what might happen to them?
(They will begin to sag when the interior begins to warm up.)

c. How do the igloo builders make sure the igloo is round?
(A round mark is formed on the ground. That mark is followed.)

d. The strongest part of an igloo is where?
(the top of the dome)

e. What is the correct word for igloo?
(iglooyak)

f. What makes certain snow better than other snow for building igloos?
(low temperature, which creates long ice crystals)

g. How do you create a perfect round circle to use as a guide for building a round igloo?
(Use a peg and string.)

h. Are all ice blocks the same size when building an igloo?
(no)

i. When the igloo is completed, why are all the outside edges trimmed smoothly?
(The edges are trimmed smoothly so that the wind doesn't erode the blocks.)

j. How are cracks in the blocks covered?
(Snow is stuffed into the cracks on the inside of the igloo and the outside.)

Nomadic Tents

a. What are nomadic tents mostly made of?
(goat hair)

b. Tents are pitched in what direction?
(toward the east or the west)

c. The roof of a nomadic tent is supported by what?
(wooden poles)

d. How is goat hair thread made?
(It is woven on looms.)

e. What is the flooring of a nomadic tent made of?
(carpet or rugs)

f. What three sections are included in a nomadic or Bedouin tent?
(kitchen, family room, and men's room)

g. What color is a nomadic tent?
(black or brown, the color of most goat hair)

h. What kind of tents are used now more than goat hair tents?
(white canvas tents)

i. Nomadic or Bedouin tents are called what other name?
(Houses of Hair)

j. What do the nomadic people use for windows in their tents?
(light coming through the goat hair threads)

Tipis

a. Tipis were homes to what type of American Indians?
(the nomadic tribes or Plains Indians)

b. Tipis were made from the skin of what animal?
(buffalo)

c. What was the frame of the tipis made of?
(wooden poles)

d. How were tipis warmed?
(by fire pits)

e. What is a travois?
(a carrier made up of tipi poles attached to the horses and dragged behind the horses)

f. Why did the women set up the tipis instead of the men?
(The men were out hunting buffalo.)

g. How was buffalo hide treated before it became a covering for the tipi?
(The inside layers of the skin were scraped away and the hide was softened by a mixture of animal parts.)

h. On the board map, point to the area where tipis were the traditional dwelling.
(the American Plains map)

i. What three natural elements did the tipi work well in?
(heat, cold, and wind)

j. What did the designs on the tipi represent?
(The personalities of the people who lived in those tents.)

Rain Forests

a. Why don't rain forest houses have walls?
(The weather never gets cold.)

b. What are the roofs of rain forest houses made of?
(palm leaves and branches)

c. Why are most of the floors off the ground?
(to keep them safer from insects, spiders, snakes, and the like)

d. Name three important natural materials used in the construction of rain forest houses.
(tree trunks, palm fronds, vines)

e. Why do rain forest houses have to be rebuilt frequently?
(The roof begins to leak and become infested with roaches, spiders, and other insects.)

f. What is the man's job in building a rain forest house?
(fetching poles and weaving leaves)

g. What is the woman's job in building a rain forest house?
(weaving and gathering leaves and vines)

h. How is a rain forest house location selected?
(Land is selected that will be safe from enemies and suitable for gardens.)

i. What is a palisade?
(A palisade is a fence of logs and vines surrounding the rain forest house or village to keep out enemies.)

j. Point to an area on a map where rain forest houses are the traditional type of dwelling. (areas near the Equator: Australia, Central America, Southeast Asia, West India)

Alternative Assessment: Use this board game as a review of facts about traditional dwellings around the world.

Activity 6

Content: Language Arts

Lesson: Creative Writing

Standard: Students will write a personal narrative or creative story.

Multiple Intelligences: Verbal/Linguistic: Students will write a story. Visual/Spatial: Students will draw a picture to accompany a story.

Materials: Writing and drawing materials

Grade Level: 3

Objective: Students will read a book and use that book to write a paragraph from the point of view of one of the characters in the book. Students will draw a picture of where they are going.

Before: Read Patricia MacLachlan's classic, *What You Know First* (New York: Harper Collins, 1995).

First: Students will make a list of the different characters in the book including the narrator, Mama, Papa, Baby, Uncle Bly, Mr. Boots, and New People.

Next: Students will select one character from the story and write a paragraph or story from the point of view of that character. Suggested point of view ideas include:

a. Saying goodbye
b. Getting ready
c. What will be missed
d. Why leaving is difficult

Then: Students will write point of view pieces and illustrate those pieces.

Finally: Students will share their pieces, then reflect upon things that they would take with them if they had to move to another place.

Alternative Assessment: Discuss or create a graph showing how moving from one location to another is similar or dissimilar among dwellers of igloos, tipis, rain forest houses, nomadic tents, and students' homes.

✔ *And now, what about five good lessons from one good book?* See if these work.

The book: Taback, Simms. (2002). *This Is the House that Jack Built.* New York: G. P. Putnam's Sons.

1. Look in the newspaper. Find five diverse advertisements of houses for sale. Discuss the similarities and differences in the design and descriptions of these houses.

2. Draw your personal view of one of these houses, including the floor plan.
3. With a partner, divide a piece of large white art paper into four even squares. Draw a house that would fit the needs of four of the following characters in Taback's book: rat, cat, dog, cow, maiden, man, judge, rooster, farmer, and artist.
4. Rewrite the book with your own characters.
5. Compare your house to the houses found on the inside cover of the book.

✔ ***Oh yes. Remember the teachable moment*** that introduced our activities in this chapter? Well, here is a little lesson to go with that idea.

Activity 7

Content: Social Studies

Lesson: Timelines

Standard: Students will use timelines to place events in chronological order.

Multiple Intelligences: Logical/Mathematical: Students will arrange the houses in which they lived in correct order. Interpersonal: Students will interview parents regarding houses in which they have lived.

Materials: Twine, clothespins

Grade Level: 2–3

Objective: Students will gather information about the houses in which they have lived. They will draw each house, write about one event that took place in the house, and display each house drawing, in chronological order, on a bulletin board or a clothesline hung across the classroom.

Before: As a class, create questions to be used to interview parents and/or grandparents about the different houses in which students have lived. Suggested questions include:

1. How many different houses or apartments have I lived in?
2. Tell me about the house I lived in when I was born.
3. What interesting thing happened to me while living in each of the houses or apartments?
4. How was each house better or worse to live in?

First: Students will use these and other questions to interview parents about houses in which they lived.

Next: Students will use that information to draw these houses and write one fact about each residence.

Then: Students will put these drawings in timeline order and display them in the room, either on a bulletin board or on string stretched across the room.

Finally: Students will discuss, write about, and/or draw their own idea of the perfect place to live.

Alternative Assessment: Students will be able to answer questions about the different houses in which they lived.

And finally, if you think *a picture is worth a thousand words,* use the *Dwelling* drawing above to engage your students in seeing, writing, drawing, or just thinking about where they live and where others around the world live as well. The activities for this drawing will work wonders for boys and girls who can get a better sense of a place called home if they can see if through color, shape, form, and design.

Activity 8

Content: Reading

Lesson: Alphabetical Order and Creative Writing

Standards: Students will access, view, and respond to visual forms. Students will use the writing process to complete a variety of writing tasks.

Multiple Intelligences: Visual/Spatial: Students will observe visual art for inspiration. Verbal/Linguistic: Students will write.

Materials: Copy of the dwellings artwork

Grade Level: 3

Objective: Students will view the dwellings artwork and place 7–8 objects seen in the drawing in alphabetical order. Students will use these object words in a creative story, either written or told.

Before: Make copies of the dwellings artwork on a piece of paper, with the drawing placed on the top of the sheet of writing paper and the bottom of the paper left blank. Students will look at the dwellings artwork and talk about the picture. Some leading reflective questions may include:

1. What would be a good title for this drawing?
2. Tell me about the family who lives in the house.
3. Where have all the animals gone?
4. Describe the weather.
5. What might have a home in the large hole in the tree?

First: On a separate sheet of paper, students will look at the dwellings artwork and make a list of all the objects they observe in the picture. The objects include a tree, a house, a mountain, snow, limbs, vines, an ant, water, a birdhouse, holes, bark, the sky, an anthill, and so on.

Next: Students will select 7 to 8 of the words and put them in alphabetical order.

Then: Students will use these words, in order, to write a creative story, poem, or factual piece.

Finally: Students will share stories.

Alternative Assessment: Using the picture as a stimulus, students will write a paragraph entitled, "The Lost Boy."

Activity 9

Content: Science

Lesson: The Seasons and Dwellings

Standard: Students will identify the seasons and their characteristics.

Multiple Intelligence: Visual/Spatial: Students will draw.

Materials: Copies of the dwellings artwork

Grade Level: K–2

Objective: Students will add personal drawings to four copies of the dwellings artwork to define the four seasons and to show how people and animals live in certain seasons.

Before: Students will review the different characteristics of the four seasons.

First: Students will create seasonal drawings on each of the four artworks by adding appropriate objects, pictures, and so on that define summer, winter, spring, and fall and also show various seasonal dwellings that might be possible in this particular drawing.

Next: Students will color each art piece appropriately to the defined season of each piece.

Then: Students will give titles to each art piece.

Finally: Students will share drawings and reflect upon why certain seasons are their favorites and how dwellings for people and animals reflect different seasons.

Alternative Assessment: Students will collate the artwork into four seasonal sections and create a season booklet including all the children's work.

Activity 10

Content: Language Arts

Lesson: Telling Stories

Standard: Students will use effective vocabulary and organization to relate information.

Multiple Intelligences: Visual/Spatial: Students will use the dwellings drawing as a stimulus for telling a story. Verbal/Linguistic: Students will tell a story. Intrapersonal: Students will reflect upon past experiences.

Materials: Copies of the dwellings drawing

Grade Level: K–3

Objective: Students will look at the drawing in this chapter and tell an original story.

Before: Students will review important aspects of telling a story.

First: Students will use the dwellings drawing as a stimulus for telling stories about animals or humans who might live in the scene in the picture.

Next: Students will relate personal stories that correspond to the original stories being told.

Then: Students will answer "What would happen if . . . " questions about the picture.

Finally: Students will reflect upon their own appreciation of the drawing.

Alternative Assessment: Students will take a drawing home and ask a family member to tell them a story that comes from viewing the drawing.

To wrap up this chapter, here is every idea you ever wanted to know about dwellings or habitats. Maybe now is the time to build interest about where people and animals live and why.

Dwellings K–3

V/L	Look at several children's books. Discuss the houses in which the characters live.	Write a story or talk about its occupants.	Write fact labels to go on the mural.	Write a short paragraph about adaptations needed to live in one of these houses.	Read several renditions of *The Three Little Pigs*.
L/M	Use wood blocks to recreate a dwelling.	Compare one of these structures to your own house.	On the overhead, use colored plastic geometric chips to create a dwelling.	Chart differences in roofs, windows, building materials, and so on.	Create a riddle or clues that go with one of the global "homes."
V/S	Draw the dwelling in which you live. Cut it out.	Cut out magazine pictures of "houses" around the world.	Create a global environmental mural. Place dwelling pictures in correct environment.	Show areas on maps where various natural materials are found.	Create centers at which the houses in the stories can be constructed.
B/K	Build birdhouses to give parents for a holiday gift.	Use boxes to create a perfect bedroom for a kid.	Use clay and craft sticks to create a house or bedroom in which you would like to live.	Go online to search for facts relating to futuristic housing.	Use various supplies to create a "dwelling of the future."
M/R	Use found objects to create different kinds of home sounds.	Perform sound effect experiences with the book *The House that Jack Built* by Simms Taback.	Use rhythmic patterns to review facts about dwellings.	Use "Twinkle, Twinkle, Little Star" to compose a song about your house.	Use the same song to compose a verse about a global "home."
Inter	Give a report on different kinds of birdhouses that attract different kinds of birds.	Research and write an interview question for the topic of dwellings.	Teach a lesson about "tents" and areas of the world in which tents are used as "homes."	Read a children's book about houses to another student.	Interview a homebuilder.
Intra	"My house is/isn't safe because _____."	"What do you think a perfect bedroom would look like for a child from another country?"	Journal about why this would be a good place to live.	"Why do we live in houses and elephants don't?"	"What would you change about the place in which you live?"
N	Bring to school samples of dwellings in which animals, wild and domesticated, live.	Watch one of the "home construction" shows on TV. Discuss raw materials.	Collect or re-create insect habitats.	How would you build a shelter if you were lost in the woods? In snow? In the desert?	Do an independent project researching natural materials used in these homes.

The activities and experiences in this grid are just a bit more difficult and can bring some challenges to your students. These ideas can be used as extension lessons or individual projects, or, in some cases, in learning centers.

Dwellings 4–6

V/L	Select a culture from another country. Research how dwellings fit into that culture.	Write a story about this misplaced dwelling.	Read any version of *This Is the House that Jack Built.*	Create an audiotape of facts about a dwelling from another culture.	Create a written plan for a social studies exhibition entitled *Dwellings.*
L/M	Create categories such as function, size, age/era, global locale, style, and environment.	Use the clues in the book to design the house.	Draw and label a blueprint of your bedroom.	Make comparisons among class blueprints.	Create a timeline of these drawings.
V/S	Gather an assortment of pictures of unusual dwellings.	Draw a picture of a dwelling. Place it in the wrong environment, (e.g., an igloo in a jungle)	Look at and compare dwellings as represented in works of art.	Collect pictures of different courthouses in these different counties.	Develop a set of architectural drawings to accompany each tape.
B/K	Create a short video or slide show documentary entitled *Wrong House, Wrong Place.*	Go online to research presidential dwellings of other countries.	Take an architectural field trip throughout your community.	Create an architectural fact board game about these courthouses.	Set up an audio center for these tapes. Include maps and other physical clues.
M/R	Write a song about the house you live in.	Use a common melody to create original lyrics about cave dwellers.	Explain the lyrics to "Home on the Range."	Write a song about this misplaced dwelling.	Collect music that might fit each dwelling. Explain your reasoning.
Inter	Create and organize the agenda for this field trip.	Lead a class discussion of safety in building structures.	As a class, research the historical significance of local dwellings.	Assume a leadership role in writing letters to county seats for information.	Write an independent report of some aspect of one of these dwellings.
Intra	"If I could live in any dwelling, it would be _____ because _____."	What materials would make up the strongest dwelling for a particular area of the world?	Think about what a house would look like in that environment. Where might it be located?	"The simplest dwelling I know is the _____."	"Why do we study dwellings?"
N	Compare a bird's nest to your home regarding materials and their functions.	Research three architectural styles from any place in the world.	Give a report on insect dwellings.	Show how an igloo or tipi works.	Show why some buildings survive hurricanes, earthquakes, floods, tornados, and so on.

EMOTIONS

Dear Teacher,

What would fear sound like if it were music? What color is pride? Are teachers ever scared? What kind of machinery could create bravery? What shape is frustration? If happiness were a food, what would it be? How do you dance anticipation?

This chapter looks at different ways of teaching and bringing attention to those personal qualities and characteristics that help make us who we are: our moods and feelings. We all have, in our early teaching experiences, sat our children in circles on the floor and called out various emotions while our boys and girls created those emotions with their faces. Some of us have even gone beyond the "mad/glad/sad/bad" collection of emotions and asked our students to increase their vocabulary of emotion words by using them on a regular basis, by writing in those emotional voices, by problem solving emotional states, by trying out new feeling words through art and movement, and by introducing, daily, one feeling word that students would be called upon to "live" as the day progressed. These, plus the four main feelings we fall back on in a pinch, are the kinds of mood and feeling experiences that will be addressed again in this chapter. Additionally, there will be several activities based on children's literature. And I can't write a chapter without at least one song included.

So, why don't we begin with a song about being scared, among other things? First off, play a common rendition of the song, "Do Re Mi," from the movie or Broadway soundtrack of *The Sound of Music*. Once students familiarize themselves with the melody, teach them these new lyrics below. As I have mentioned quite often in this book, there are many karaoke tapes that can be used in the classroom in the most wonderful of ways. Some of these tapes, of course, include the "Do Re Mi" melody. My personal bible for finding karaoke tapes of all kinds is the Sound Choice Cassette and CDG catalog of karaoke tapes. Visit them online at www.soundchoice.com, or write to Sound Choice, 14100 South Lakes Drive, Charlotte, NC 28273 to order an updated catalog.

Now, here is the song. This melody is so well known by most students that you don't even need an accompanying music tape. Just go for it!

S-c-a-r-e-d

(Tune: "Do, Re, Mi" from *The Sound of Music*)

I was scared, so very scared
when I heard a little noise.
Was it something that had teeth
or gigantic, pointed claws?
What was I supposed to do?

Be a chicken and go, "shoo"?
Grab a stick and holler, "boo"?
I was very, very s-c-a-r-e-d.
Soon a plan began to grow
deep inside my little head.
First, I'd turn the lights on bright
then look underneath my bed.
And, you know, that's what I did.
Slowly, I am just a kid.
There it was, the thing that hid.
What a little, bitty thing.
Just my kitty wrapped in yarn
tightly wound around her neck.
So I gently pulled her out,
kitty scratches, what the heck.
Now she's safe and I am pleased.
Cats are more fun when they breathe.
I will call it my good deed,
and to think that I was
A little, scaredy, scaredy cat.

Or if you have a soft place in your hearts for dogs instead of cats, teach your students this doggy-oriented lyric about nervousness.

N-e-r-v-o-u-s

(Tune: "Do, Re, Mi")

I'm a little spotted dog.
Nothing fancy, I must say.
I've got hair all in my eyes
But it's never in the way.
I can bark and bring on fear
and my legs run far and near.
But when people pet my ears
I get very, very n-e-r-v-o-u-s.
I begin to pout and moan
Then I shiver up a storm
Please don't try to pull my ears
I will cause myself some harm
I can feel the shaking start
Nerves don't help this little heart
I don't want to break apart
I am very, very n-e-r-v-o-u-s
Now my breathing's slowing down
No one's touched my ears this time.
I get up and find my tail.
It's still where it was. How fine.

Soon I scamper down the street
dodging yet another sweet
little girl who wants to greet
my nervous, nervous ears.
Please never, ever pull my ears.

Songs and lyrics can be marvelous introductions to any content area and specific lesson, including emotions and feelings. As an addendum to the songs and lyrics in this chapter introduction, you may wish to do simple beginning experiences with your boys and girls once they have finished singing these two verses. General ideas like these below will open up more interesting interactions between your children and the moods they might find themselves in or the emotions they may be feeling as certain situations dictate.

1. Have personal discussions about times children were nervous or scared.
2. Ask questions about the lyrics. For example, why do some dogs not like having their ears touched or pulled? Or, what one thing about cats frightens you?
3. Make a list of words that mean the same as nervousness or fear. Use those words in sentences.

Finally, sing the verses with the children again. Change a few of the words in the lyrics. Don't worry about the rhyming effect. Discuss how the changing of a few words may, in fact, change the mood of the verse. Later on, this information will be put to use when the students write stories or paragraphs in certain voices or points of view, create descriptive words to enrich their writing, or simply come to a situation in school in which they have to engage in personal problem-solving techniques with other students.

This particular chapter concentrates heavily on kindergarten and first grade; thus, many of the activities are bodily/kinesthetic in nature as that is how children of this age make the best and clearest sense of things: through manipulation and movement. With just an adaptive touch here and there, these same activities can be developmentally correct for older children also. However, the activities that accompany the *Emotions* drawing at the end of the chapter work exceptionally well for those students in second and third grades and into the intermediate grade levels.

You really don't want to go to work this morning, so you think of an excuse to give the school secretary when you call to tell her you are not coming in. This frustrates you having to wait until 6 A.M., as you are already up and have the excuse in your head. You go downstairs to the kitchen and step on a dog toy. This angers you and you want to throw the dog toy out the window with the dog, but you are a little nervous about doing this since the dog would look pitiful and, of course, that would make you feel immensely sorry for the little critter. You are anxious for 6 to come because once you call your excuse in, you will feel so much more relaxed. The dread that you often feel when you do these kinds of things will go away and you can plan your day. That will make you happy, so you anticipate what adventure you might soon plan. A feeling of confusion overtakes you, however, as you realize that you should probably go to school today.

You sigh a long sigh of consternation, but then you suddenly feel peaceful. School is where you belong today. And in an instant, you have the makings of a brilliant lesson on moods and emotions. A teachable moment has joyfully entered your life, and you are ever so pleased.

Activity 1

Content: Social Studies

Lesson: Emotion Cards

Standard: Students will recognize various ways of feeling.

Multiple Intelligence: Visual/Spatial: Students will look at different drawings.

Materials: Paper plates, crayons

Grade Level: K

Objective: Students will look at different faces drawn or pasted on paper plates. Students will select appropriate moods or feelings that go with the different faces.

Before: Read the following phrases. Students will discuss feelings or emotions that come from these sentences.

1. Sick puppy
2. Taking a test
3. Going to the zoo
4. Having the measles
5. Sliding down the slide
6. Hearing a joke
7. Getting a kitten out of a tree
8. Lost in the woods

9. Earning an A on a spelling test

10. Waiting a turn at bat

11. Being grounded

12. Losing your temper

13. Loud crash

First: On the chalkboard, place a list of emotions that come from the responses from the above phrases. Add other emotion words as discussions warrant such as surprise, anxiety, courage, disappointment, anger, pride, and so on.

Next: Students will use this list and other emotion words they discover to create emotion faces on paper places. Each student may choose four emotions in order to make four paper plate faces.

Then: Read the following story. When the symbol ⊕ appears, stop reading so that students may hold up an appropriate paper plate emotion face at that appropriate part of the story. Disregard the underlined words for the moment. They have to do with the alternative assessment at the end of this activity.

The Three Ugly Mice

Once upon a time there lived, in a barn on a farm, three mice. They were so <u>ugly</u> and <u>frightful</u> looking ⊕ that when they went into the barnyard to <u>steal</u> food or look for a place to sleep, the chickens would run and hide under the nearest haystack ⊕. When the three mice strolled into the barn to look for bits of corn, the horses would <u>crouch</u> down behind their stalls and cover their heads with feed <u>buckets</u> ⊕. And when the three mice wandered into the fields <u>searching</u> for cousins to play with, the cows would roll over on their backs and <u>giggle</u> until their sides <u>ached</u> ⊕. Even the cousins ran away, laughing so hard they <u>cried</u> ⊕.

This kind of <u>behavior</u> upset the three mice very much ⊕, for they could not understand why the animals were acting that way ⊕. You see, the three mice did not know they were ugly. In fact, their parents had told them that they were the prettiest mice ever to be born ⊕. This made the three mice very <u>happy</u> ⊕. So they never <u>worried</u> ⊕ about a thing.

One day as the three mice played hide and seek in the barn loft, they heard a strange <u>crackling</u> noise. The noise made them <u>scamper</u>, quickly, into a hole in the floor of the loft. "We must see what is causing this noise," said one of the mice. They took a deep breath, stood up straight and tall, and <u>peeked</u> out ⊕. Looking between the cracks of the loft floor, what they saw made them <u>tremble</u> ⊕. A wall of fire ⊕!

"Hurry!" they shouted to each other. "We must get the animals out of the barn. We must save them." So the three mice ran down into the barn and squeaked their loudest, <u>darted</u> their fastest, and climbed up and down and around the other animals to get them to run out of the barn. And out the animals ran, <u>shrieking</u> ⊕, <u>shaking</u> ⊕, <u>laughing</u> ⊕, and mumbling ⊕ out the doors of the barn, into the barnyard and safety.

"Whoa!" they all cried. "What was that about?" "Where are those three mice?" "Let me get my hands on them" ⊕. And all the other farm animals began to walk toward the three mice, who were in the corner of the barnyard, trembling ⊕. "Wait a minute," said one of the pigs, who was slowly crawling out of a hole full of water. "I think they saved our lives. Look!" he yelled ⊕. "The barn is on fire."

The other animals looked toward the barn just as the roof <u>collapsed</u> in flames. They all <u>shrank</u> back in horror ⊕. "We would have been killed!" they all screamed. "The three mice saved our lives." The animals looked at each other and then toward the three mice that were still sitting in the corner of the barnyard, trembling ⊕. "You are our heroes!" the animals shouted ⊕ as they ran to the mice.

    So with that, they picked up the three mice, put them on the back of the largest horse on the farm, and had a <u>parade</u> ⊕ celebrating their good fortune. And from that day on, the three mice lived happily among all the farm animals, who were <u>kind</u> and <u>considerate</u> and thought the three mice were the most beautiful creatures in the whole wide world.

Finally: Students will reflect, through drawings, upon personal feelings of sadness, happiness, and feelings of being made fun of.

Alternative Assessment: Students will think of other words to place into the story instead of the ones that are underlined.

Activity 2

Content: Language Arts, Math

Lesson: Teddy Bears and Problem Solving

Standard: Students will choose the best course of action through problem solving.

Multiple Intelligence: Bodily/Kinesthetic: Students will manipulate teddy bears to formulate mood scenes.

Materials: Teddy bears

Grade Level: K–1

Objective: Students will listen to a children's book and then create mood scenes that dictate different moods.

Before: Students will bring stuffed teddy bears to class.

First: Students will listen to the children's book *Worry Bear* by Charlotte Dematons (Asheville, NC: Front Street and Lerninscaat, 2002).

Next: Students will use their teddy bears to create scenes that incorporate different moods and emotions.

Then: Students will relate events in which they have lost their tempers and become very angry. Students will use teddy bear scenarios to problem solve those events.

Finally: Students will divide a piece of art paper into two sections. In one section, they will draw their own meaning of "anger." In the other section, they will draw their own meaning of "happiness."

Alternative Assessment: Students will look in other children's books for evidence of the emotion of *anger* and discuss their findings.

Activity 3

Content: Language Arts

Lesson: Paper Dolls and Loneliness

Standards: Students will follow simple directions. Students will describe needs, wants, and feelings.

Multiple Intelligence: Visual/Spatial: Students will make and design paper dolls. Students will listen to and discuss a children's book.

Materials: Construction paper, glue, scissors, cardboard sheets

Grade Level: K–2

Objective: Students will listen to a children's book. Students will design and cut out paper doll clothes that make a scarecrow not so scary.

Before: Draw a shape that represents the human form. Duplicate this shape onto cardstock or cardboard sheets. Cut these shapes out or, depending on developmental capabilities, have students use scissors to cut them out.

First: Read *The Lonely Scarecrow* by Tim Preston, illustrated by Maggie Keen (New York: Dutton Children's Books, 2002).

Next: Discuss and brainstorm what the scarecrow can do to become less lonely. Lead the conversation toward these suggestions:

1. Take the scarecrow to the beach.
2. Take the scarecrow to a football, baseball, or basketball game.
3. Take him to see his grandmother or grandfather.
4. Bake the scarecrow a cake.

Then: Students will use the cardboard human shape as a pattern for making clothes that will "take him to a place" where he won't be lonely, like the beach, a football game, and so on.

Finally: Students will use these clothed patterns to discuss and reflect upon personal scenarios of loneliness.

Alternative Assessment: Students will use a combination of patterned shapes as catalysts for creating original stories about feelings of loneliness and other feelings.

Activity 4

Content: Language Arts, Visual Arts

Lesson: Clay and Emotions

Standard: Students will use art media to communicate ideas, experiences, and stories.

Multiple Intelligence: Bodily/Kinesthetic: Students will create objects from clay.

Materials: Clay, art paper, children's book

Grade Level: K–1

Objective: Students will listen to a children's book and use their bodies to show the feeling of bravery.

Before: Find an open floor space that allows students the ability to move around. Call out an emotion. Students will move around the room defining that emotion with their bodies.

First: Read *Brave Mole* by Lynne Jonell (New York: G. P. Putnam's Sons, 2002).

Next: Read the book again. On the second reading, students will move their bodies as the text warrants.

Then: Students will brainstorm scenarios in which bravery is required. Volunteers will pantomime or show bravery in movement. Other students will guess the event.

Finally: Students will reflect on this question: "A family member was brave once when he or she _____."

Alternative Assessment: Students will listen to other children's stories about bravery. They will make comparisons.

Activity 5

Content: Language Arts, Math

Lesson: Emotion Chart

Standard: Students will construct, read, and interpret displays of data.

Multiple Intelligence: Logical/Mathematical: Students will gather data and create a chart.

Materials: Chart paper

Grade Level: 1–3

Objective: Students will listen to two children's books. They will gather information regarding different emotions. Students will analyze these emotions and compare them in a chart format.

Before: Read *Today Is Feel Silly and Other Moods that Make My Day* by Jamie Lee Curtis, illustrated by Laura Cornell (New York: Joanna Cotler Books, an imprint of Harpercollins, 1998); and *I Was Silly* by Marci Curtis (New York: Dial Books for Young Readers, 2002).

First: Students will create individual charts such as the one on the following page.

They will look in both books for evidence of these emotions and others. Students will write down different ways the emotions were expressed under the appropriate book titles.

Next: Students will think of times in which they felt these certain emotions. These events will be placed under the "Self" column.

Feelings	Today is Feel Silly & Other Moods That Make My Day	I Was Silly	Self
Silly			
Excited			
Discouraged			
Frustrated			
Naughty			
Scary			
Smart			
Angry			

Then: Students will discuss similarities and differences among the three columns.

Finally: Students will reflect upon the one emotion they have trouble handling or the one event in which they were the silliest.

Alternative Assessment: Students will define certain feelings with their own faces or bodies as the teacher calls out the emotions written on the chart.

Activity 6

Content: Music

Lesson: Defining Emotions through Music

Standard: Students will identify music that creates changes in mood through listening examples.

Multiple Intelligences: Musical/Rhythmic: Students will listen to music. Interpersonal: Students will teach a lesson.

Materials: Selection of taped music

Grade Level: 3

Objective: Students will listen to a tape of combined music of different genres and moods. Students will discuss emotions instilled by listening to the music. Students will also discuss what emotion the music sounds like.

Before: Find a selection of music that elicits different emotions. Make a tape of that music.

First: Play each cut of music. Students will discuss the emotion that comes to mind when listening to that cut. They will also discuss the different sounds and instruments of each cut and the relationship of those sounds and instruments (loud, soft, strings, brass, drums, and so on) to various feelings.

Next: As an assignment, students in groups will create a tape of three song selections.

Then: Students will teach a mood-related lesson to the rest of the class using the three-song tape as the focal point of the lesson.

Finally: Students will reflect upon the importance of music to feelings by discussing their favorite music and why it makes them happy, excited, calm, and so on.

Alternative Assessment: Listen to all kinds of songs. Students will select one mood elicited from one cut of music. Students will create an album cover to go with the song.

✔ *And now, what about the five good lessons from one good book?* See if these work.

The book: Smith, Lane. (1996). *Flying Jake.* New York: Aladdin Books.

1. Look at this wordless picture book. Create an improvisational story to go along with the illustrations.
2. Students will pick a character from the book, animate or inanimate. They will read the book again, using the illustrations as a guide. The different characters seen in each frame will tell the story. The story will be told in the first person.
3. At the end of the storytelling, students will discuss the different moods and emotions their characters felt as the story progressed.
4. Students will use the illustrations from only one page to tell a brief, complete story that clearly shows one emotion.
5. One student or the teacher will "tell" the story as other class members pantomime the action of the characters.

✔ *Oh yes. Remember the teachable moment* that introduced our activities in this chapter? Well, here is a little lesson to go with that idea.

Activity 7

Content: Language Arts

Lesson: Emotions and Poetry

Standard: Students will use correct conventions: spelling, punctuation, grammar, word usage, and penmanship.

Multiple Intelligence: Verbal/Linguistic: Students will make lists and write poems.

Materials: None

Grade Level: 3

Objective: Students will write down the significant emotions they feel at any given time during the course of a week. Students will use these emotions to write poems.

Before: Students will create a booklet of blank pages in which to keep a clear record of significant emotions and feelings felt during the course of a week.

First: Students will learn the formula for writing cinquains and will practice writing them. The cinquain format below can be placed on chart paper as a reminder for children while they write their own poems.

Line 1: one word—title

Line 2: two words—describes title

Line 3: three words—shows action relating to title

Line 4: four words—shows feeling relating to title

Line 5: one word—synonym of title

The following emotion cinquain can be used as a sample.

Fear

Big, black

Jumping from behind

Like an angry bear

Scared

Next: Students will select one emotion and write a cinquain.

Then: Students will share their poems and display them on a wall in the classroom.

Finally: Students will reflect upon the emotion they felt during the last week that was the most surprising to them.

Alternative Assessment: Students may illustrate their cinquains or perform, verbally or nonverbally, the poems.

✓ And finally, if you think *a picture is worth a thousand words,* use the *Emotions* drawing on the previous page to engage your students in seeing, writing, drawing, or just thinking about how they feel at any given time, at any given moment. The activities that accompany this drawing will work wonders for boys and girls who are able to use various experiences in school as a way of getting in touch with their emotions, and who have a clearer understanding of these feelings through color, shape, form, and design.

Activity 8

Content: Math

Lesson: Before and after Predictions

Standard: Students will predict the likelihood of events.

Multiple Intelligences: Visual/Spatial: Students will use a drawing as a stimulus. Logical/Mathematical: Students will make predictions.

Materials: Copies of the emotions drawing

Grade Level: 2–3

Objective: Students will look at a drawing and make predictions about feelings and emotions.

Before: Role-play two or three scenarios in which students look at scenes and make predictions of how the scenes will end or what might transpire immediately before or after the scenes. Sample scenarios are:

1. A desk that has been turned over on the floor
2. A deflated basketball
3. A missing coat on a line of coat racks or hangers filled with coats
4. A sheet on which is written the letters of the alphabet with one letter missing

First: Make an overhead transparency of the emotions drawing, or give each student a copy of the drawing.

Next: Have students look at the first picture of the man on the top line of the drawing. Students will look at the drawing of the man and discuss what he might be doing, saying, or feeling. Students will draw a picture in the blank space to the right of the picture to show what the man may be feeling next.

Then: Students will use this "before" and "after" format to complete three of the pictures in the drawing.

Finally: Students will share their drawings of *before* and *after* predictions.

Alternative Assessment: Students will take the emotions drawing home and complete the rest of the pictures with the help of their family members.

Activity 9

Content: Language Arts

Lesson: Complete Sentences

Standard: Students will use correct conventions: spelling, punctuation, grammar, word usage, and penmanship.

Multiple Intelligence: Verbal/Linguistic: Students will write complete sentences.

Materials: Copies of emotions drawing

Grade Level: 1–3

Objective: Students will use the emotions drawing to write complete sentences that focus on how the characters in the drawings feel.

Before: Ask three students to come to the front of the room. Each student will make some kind of face that depicts a feeling. Other students will look at the faces and say complete sentences for each face that tells what the students might be feeling. Sample sentences may include:

1. Angry face: "I broke my pencil and am so mad."
2. Shy face: "Please don't ask me to read outloud."
3. Grumpy face: "I'm hungry."

First: Students will look at the emotions drawing and volunteer to make a complete sentence, orally, for one of the faces on the drawing.

Next: Students will use the spaces on either side of three drawings to write a complete sentence that tells a feeling the drawings depict.

Then: Students will take one picture at a time and share their complete sentences. They may wish to write them on the board.

Finally: Circle the students on the floor. One at a time, they will show a face. Volunteers will create a complete sentence about what emotion or feeling that face depicts.

Alternative Assessment: Draw an original face on art paper. Other students will write a complete sentence to go with the original face.

Activity 10

Content: Visual Arts, Math, and Language Arts

Lesson: Emotion Bingo

Standards: Students will identify realistic art. Students will interpret displays of information. Students will use games to identify and count. Students will listen and respond to sentences.

Multiple Intelligence: Logical/Mathematical: Students will formulate ideas about correct answers. Students will use images to problem solve.

Materials: Copies of emotions drawing

Grade Level: K–1

Objective: Students will choose correct emotion faces by playing a game.

Before: Play "Show Me" with the class. Call out a feeling or emotion word. Students will define that word with an appropriate facial expression. Suggested words are happy, frightened, tired, mean, goofy, nice, and upset.

First: Distribute emotions drawings to all the children. Read the following sentences. Using the emotions drawings, students will place tokens on the correct facial expressions represented.

1. The little girl was so *cheerful* that she sang a happy song.
2. When the little boy lost his dog, he thought his *heart would break.*
3. When the man went to cut the lawn, he got so hot he became very *thirsty.*
4. Timmy was in *love.*
5. When Eric went into the cave, he heard a noise that *surprised* him.
6. Sam did not know the answer to the question and felt very *goofy.*
7. Billy *lost his temper* when he couldn't find his wallet.
8. Mary Elizabeth became very *shy* when someone told her how beautiful she was.
9. Matthew felt *good* when he knew how to spell the word.
10. The old man was *calm* and very *quiet* as he listened to the story.
11. When he got caught stealing a cat, the boy felt very *stupid.*
12. Look at the last picture on the drawing. What kind of feeling is this man having?

Next: Students will look at the unused picture on the drawing and create a complete sentence that shows an appropriate feeling the man may be having.

Then: Students will discuss the various faces and the emotions they think are represented.

Finally: Students will talk about the different moods they have been in at school this day or week, and why the moods were prevalent.

Alternative Assessment: Students will draw a picture that describes one of the moods they were in during the day or week.

Activity 11

Content: Arts

Lesson: Drawing Feelings, Dancing Feelings

Standards: Students will use art to express ideas and feelings. Students will present and discuss varying interpretations of ideas. Students will identify music that creates changes in moods through listening examples.

Multiple Intelligences: Bodily/Kinesthetic: Students will create movement pieces. Visual/Spatial: Students will draw. Musical/Rhythmic: Students will use appropriate music as catalysts for dancing.

Materials: Copies of the emotions drawing, various pieces of mood music

Grade Level: K–3

Objective: Students will draw facial expressions and create emotion movements to accompany the facial expressions.

Before: Students will draw different emotional expressions in the blank spaces of the emotions drawing.

First: Students will discuss the new drawings and how they relate or compare to other drawings of similar expressions in the emotions drawing.

Next: Students will select one new drawing and create whole body movements that define the emotion described in the drawing. Students will demonstrate those movements after listening to and choosing various selections of music at hand.

Then: Students will discuss each other's efforts and give positive feedback.

Finally: Students will reflect upon the use of movement and music as ways of showing how they feel at certain times.

Alternative Assessment: Play selections of music. Students will discuss the moods that the selections create in them.

Activity 12

Content: Language Arts

Lesson: Add-on Story

Standards: Students will listen and respond to stories. Students will use effective vocabulary to relate information.

Multiple Intelligence: Verbal/Linguistic: Students will listen and speak.

Materials: Copies of emotions drawing

Grade Level: K–1

Objective: Students will listen as a story is being read. Students will use complete sentences to add to the story.

Before: Review the different emotions found on the faces in the emotions drawing.

First: Read the following short story. As it is read, students will fill in the blanks by orally adding appropriate sentences of their own. They will look at the emotions drawing for context clues.

> There once was a young girl who liked to whistle. When she whistled, she felt like _____. One day, she walked passed a boy who was crying. "Why are you crying?" she asked. The young boy said, "I am crying because _____." The young girl said, "Then come with me." So off they went.

The two walked for a while until they met a young girl with long hair. "Why are your eyes closed?" the whistling girl asked. "I become very shy when _____," the beautiful girl said. "That is why I keep my eyes closed." "Then come with me," said the whistling girl. And the three continued to walk down the street.

Soon they spotted a boy who was wearing a mask. "Why are you wearing a mask?" the whistling girl asked. "My bad-looking teeth make me feel embarrassed," the masked boy said. "So, if I wear a mask _____," he said softly. "Then come with me," the whistling girl said. And the four walked arm in arm together.

The group soon spied a man with a wide-open mouth. "Why is your mouth open?" the whistling girl asked. "Why, something just ran out of those bushes and surprised me," the man said. "What do you think it was?" asked the whistling girl. "Oh, I am sure it was _____," the surprised man said. "Then come with me," said the whistling girl. And the five walked arm and arm down the street.

They walked and walked until they spotted a boy who looked hot and sweaty. "Why are you so hot?" the whistling girl asked. "I have just _____," the boy replied, "and I need something to cool me off."

The five friends looked at each other. "We are hot, too," they said at the same time. So they all sat down and drank big glasses of icy, cold _____. "This makes me feel _____," they all said, and soon big smiles spread over all their faces because _____. And they continued to go, arm in arm, on their merry way.

Next: Ask students to retell the story in their own words.

Then: Students may choose any art media (drawing, water colors, clay, newspaper sculpture, geometric cut-out shapes, and so on) to recreate the scene in the story.

Finally: Students will title the story and discuss why they chose their particular titles.

Alternative Assessment: Students will use their recreated art pieces to write their own stories.

Activity 13

Content: Language Arts

Lesson: Telling Stories

Standard: Students will use effective vocabulary and organization to relate information.

Multiple Intelligences: Visual/Spatial: Students will use the emotions drawing as a stimulus for telling a story. Verbal/Linguistic: Students will tell a story. Intrapersonal: Students will reflect upon past experiences.

Materials: Copies of the emotions drawing

Grade Level: K–3

Objective: Students will look at the drawing in this chapter and tell an original story.

Before: Students will review important aspects of telling a story.

First: Students will use the emotions drawing as a stimulus for telling stories about other humans who might belong in the drawing.

Next: Students will relate personal stories that correspond to the original stories being told.

Then: Students will answer "What would happen if..." questions about the picture.

Finally: Students will reflect upon their own appreciation of the drawing.

Alternative Assessment: Students will take a drawing home and ask a family member to tell them a story that comes from viewing the drawing.

To wrap up this chapter, here is every idea you ever wanted to know about emotions. Maybe now is the time for students to get a feel for what they are learning.

Emotions K–3

V/L	Read *Sheila Rae, the Brave*, by Kevin Hankes.	Discuss what to do if you get lost on your way home from school.	Describe what your heart does when you experience different emotions.	Read *On Monday When it Rained*, by Cheryl Kachenmeister.	Write about these pictures.
L/M	Create a "sound" chart of various emotions.	Create cause-and-effect scenarios about fear.	Use geometric shapes on the overhead to create story problems about anger.	Create a chart of moods and explicit instances when you have those moods.	Form opinions of what makes people angry.
V/S	Draw what those sounds might look like.	Show a broad array of pictures that possibly evoke feelings of bravery, fear, or pride.	Use pictures to create collages depicting certain emotions.	Create a tactile book of moods. Use various textures to show these moods or emotions.	Design a book to accompany these pictures.
B/K	Take a walk about the school. Observe locations where courage is required.	Create an original puppet play using various emotions as characters.	Work with students in higher grades to create a outdoor game about emotions.	Take photos of students showing different emotional faces.	Pantomime moods and emotions using your own shadows.
M/R	Make up songs to go with the collages.	Use various musical pieces to chart different emotions.	Reread *Sheila Rae, the Brave*. Create sound and motions to characterize parts of the book.	Sing the song, "S-c-a-r-e-d." Pay attention to pitch and tone.	Listen to songs written about accomplishments.
Inter	In groups, create a newspaper sculpture that denotes pride.	Interview teachers about their proudest moments.	Create a bulletin board to showcase good deeds.	Brainstorm ways to show pride in your work.	Create a "Good Deed Tree." Each leaf describes one good deed by students.
Intra	"The scariest I have ever been in my life was when ____."	Write a journal entry about helping others and the feeling that comes from that.	"The bravest think I ever did was ____." Draw the moment.	What does "fear smells" mean?	"I'm silly when I ____."
N	How does fear help people survive certain situations?	Investigate fact or fiction accounts of animal bravery.	Identify fearful things in nature.	Describe ways water is helpful or harmful. Connect this to fear and bravery.	Investigate ways pets show emotions such as fear, happiness, and anger.

The activities and experiences in this grid are just a bit more difficult and can bring some challenges to your students. These ideas can be used as extension lessons, individual projects, or, in some cases, in learning centers.

Emotions 4–6

V/L	Write a poem about a mood.	Read sections of juvenile books that describe various moods.	Interview different age groups. Ask them to define certain emotions.	Discuss particular passages.	Write an original story about a brave event.
L/M	Using only five straight lines, illustrate fear, bravery, silliness, and anger.	Use objects (rocks, toothpicks, craft sticks) to create problem-solving scenes re: moods.	Keep track of times during the week you show pride.	Do the same with transparency geometric shapes.	Analyze your own responses to certain role-play situations.
V/S	Look at well-known works of art for "mood."	Create works of art through your personal eye and personal experience.	Draw a picture to be used as a clue for a role-play scene.	Use found objects to create a sculpture of one emotion or mood.	Use guided imagery to create a mood scenario.
B/K	Role-play student-related situations involving certain moods.	Act out historical scenes that depict certain mood events. (e.g., bravery, pride.)	Perform as a play or pantomime.	Use different hats as catalysts for creating spontaneous scenes.	Create a video documentary.
M/R	Write new lyrics with an existing melody about frustration.	Collect sound effects that do the same.	Use karaoke tapes to retell these scenes through music.	Create an emotion rap.	Learn a song from parents or grandparents that "soothed" them as children.
Inter	Volunteer to call someone to be a guest speaker in class. Topic: heroic acts (firefighters, etc.)	Recognize and validate "good deeds" of peers.	Give oral report of cowardly acts in history.	Collect stories of heroism from local newspaper. Give report of your findings.	Volunteer to go to lower grades to read stories about bravery, fear, and the like.
Intra	"I sometimes get a little goose-bumpy" when I _____.	"If fear were a color, it would be _____." How would it taste?	"The bravest person I know is _____ because_____."	"Music adds a lot to a scary movie because _____."	"At night when it is dark and I am in my bed, I sometimes get scared when _____."
N	How do animals, wild or domesticated, show fear? Compare this to humans.	When walking home today, look at a part of nature that pleases or scares.	Investigate examples of children and bravery.	Investigate survival stories.	Why does certain weather evoke fear?

HANDS

Dear Teacher,

My job as an educator and writer of books is to use interesting and seldom tried strategies that might engage, expand, and excite students in the learning process. This chapter focuses on a teaching tool that is seen in the classroom daily, and used, although in simple utilitarian ways, on a daily basis as well. I am talking about hands. So, the next few pages will take us away from seeing hands as mere functional appendages for holding pencils, getting attention, knowing an answer, counting, grasping doorknobs, or scooting back chairs. Instead, we are going to see hands as catalysts for understanding specific elements and teaching standards found in social studies and language arts curricula.

Teachable moments come at the strangest times and in even stranger places. Several years ago, I came across a whimsical little book in an art store in San Francisco. I was mesmerized by its title, *Hands: A Pictoral Archive from Nineteenth-Century Sources— 1166 Copyright-free Illustrations for Artists and Designers*, selected by Jim Harter (New York: Dover Publications, 1985). I was even more mesmerized by its contents: pen and ink drawings of hands and all kinds of hands doing all kinds of things. This one little ninety-page book created a faucet of ideas for me and has been instrumental in my constructing purposeful experiences for boys and girls in a classroom setting.

I've recently discovered that Dover Publications has a collection of these types of books that focus on copyright-free illustrations of animals, children, food and drink, and music. I feel another chapter coming on.

To begin the connection with hands and purpose, students must see their hands in a different light. Therefore, the first lesson of the day is an easy one. The students will simply compare their hands.

Use a long strip of either white or black butcher paper. Place the paper on a table and have the kids, five at a time, place their right hands on the paper, palms down. The five students will then compare their hands according to:

Size

Color

Oddities

Freckles

Scars

Length

Other

Students will then turn their right hands over and do likewise, comparing hands according to:

Lines

Dimensions

Length of fingers

Thumbs

Creases

Other

End this short exercise with a reflective question. Ask each student when, during the day, they like their hands the best. Wrap up this first episode with a little homework assignment. Students will follow their hands around until bedtime. They will come back the next morning and discuss one thing they saw their hand(s) do. After this discussion, writing a paragraph about this event can't be too far away.

You jump in the car and make a mad dash for the grocery store, where you will pick up another bulb of garlic you need for the pasta dinner tonight. As you drive, you inadvertently look down at your hands that are clutching the steering wheel. For a moment, you see what appears to be a small fly resting lazily on the top of your right hand. As you try to shake it off you realize that it is, in fact, not a fly but a brown spot. With an unblinking stare at the brown spot, you begin to notice that somewhere during the last few days or weeks, someone has attached your mother's hands onto your wrists without your permission. "Oh, my goodness," you call out to no one in particular. "When did this happen?" Then you begin to think about it all, and as you dodge the truck in the lane next to you, you wonder if your mother's hands looked like her mother's hands, and if your grandmother's hands looked like her mother's hands. You look at your two hands and a comfortable smile works its way across your face. And in an instant, you have the makings of a brilliant lesson on hands. A teachable moment has placed itself into your life, and you are ever so pleased.

Activity 1

Content: Language Arts

Lesson: Following Simple Directions

Standard: Students will follow simple directions.

Multiple Intelligence: Bodily/Kinesthetic: Students will use their hands to demonstrate certain actions.

Materials: White gloves

Grade Level: K–3

Objective: The students will listen to a group of phrases and demonstrate the meaning of those phrases by following directions and acting out those phrases with their hands.

Before: Give students a few of the following verbal directions that must be accomplished by using, first, their feet.

Stand still	Walk five steps	Cross your feet
Walk backwards	Stand on one foot	Stand on tiptoes
Spin on one foot	Walk sideways	Hop three times

First: Ask students to listen to the following phrases and use their hands to demonstrate the meaning of the phrases.

Throw hands away	Shake hands	Show strong hands
Show weak hands	Show a witch's hands	Show a giant's hands
Show a snake climbing a tree	Show a caterpillar lying on a leaf	Show a dog burying a bone
Show a squirrel holding a nut	Climb a rope	Read a book
Hold a baby	Show the talons of an eagle	Keep warm
Beg for food	Hold a flower	Show surprise
Show your mother's hands	Show your hands	Show your father's hands

Next: Read the following story to the class. Students will use their hands to act out the above phrases, which have been imbedded in the story.

The Boy Who Loved His Hands

Once upon a time, there was young boy who loved to look at his hands. When he tried to *read a book,* he often lost his place because he was too busy staring at his hands. When he was in the backyard playing on the old rope tied to a tree, he sometimes had trouble *climbing the rope* because he was always staring at his hands. One time when he was being introduced to a friend of his mother's, he forgot to *shake hands* with the woman because, you guessed it: he was too busy staring at his hands.

He also loved to play pretend with his hands. For example, sometimes he pretended that he could unhook his hands from his wrists and *throw his hands away.* Sometimes as he walked home from school, he pretended he had really *strong hands,* and he would roar and make his hands look like the large hands *of a giant.* Sometimes he pretended to have really *weak hands* and made believe that he was a tiny, baby squirrel trying to *hold a nut.*

One Saturday as he walked with his mom and dad to the park near his home, he stopped by a tree and used his hands to show a *snake climbing a tree.* He even got down on the ground by the path and used his finger to show what a *caterpillar might look like lying on a leaf.*

Yes, the young boy loved to look at his hands, especially when he pretended to *hold a flower* to give to the teacher . . . and watch her hold her hands up to her face . . . with *surprise.*

Then: Ask children to think of ways they use their hands such as dressing themselves for school, or eating an ice cream cone, or riding their bikes. Students will think of one way they use their hands. Each child will use the following sentence to incorporate his or her word into a request for the other children to follow directions: "I use my hand(s) to _____ (dry off my dog when he gets wet). With your hand(s), show me three ways to _____ (dry off your dog when he gets wet)."

Finally: Students will use the following supplemental sheet of the above story and fill in their own ways of telling the story using their hands.

The Boy Who Loved His Hands

Once upon a time, there was a young boy who loved to look at his *hands*. When he tried to _____, he often lost his place because he was too busy staring at his *hands*. When he was in the backyard playing on the old rope tied to a tree, he sometimes had trouble _____ because he was always staring at his *hands*. One time when he was being introduced to a friend of his mother's, he forgot to _____ because, you guessed it: he was too busy staring at his *hands*.

He also loved to play pretend with his *hands*. Like, for example, sometimes he pretended that he could unhook his *hands* from his wrists and _____. Sometimes as he walked home from school, he pretended he had really _____ *hands*, and he would roar and make his *hands* look like the large hands of a _____. Sometimes he pretended to have really _____ *hands* and made believe that he was a tiny, baby _____ trying to _____ a _____.

One Saturday as he walked with his mom and dad to the park near his home, he stopped by a tree and used his *hands* to show a _____. He even got down on the ground by the path and used his finger to show _____.

Yes, the young boy loved to look at his *hands*, especially when he pretended to hold a _____ to give to the teacher . . . and watch her hold her *hands* up to her face . . . with _____.

Alternative Assessment: Using construction paper, students will draw an outline of their own hands. On each finger and thumb, they will write down one useful action they can do with their hand(s) to help Mom and Dad. The hand "coupon" will be given to Mom and/or Dad as a gift. Useful actions may include washing dishes, making the bed, taking out the trash, writing Grandma, and so on.

Activity 2

Content: Language Arts

Lesson: Narrative Pantomime

Standard: Students will listen and respond to stories, poems, and nonfiction.

Multiple Intelligence: Bodily/Kinethestics: Students will use their hands to enhance an understanding of characters in a story.

Materials: White gloves

Grade Level: K–3

Objective: Students will listen as a two-character story is being read to them. As the story is being read, they will use their two hands to act out the movements of each character.

Before: Show various pictures of field mice. Lead a discussion on physical characteristics, habitat, and so on. Students may wish to research field mice on the Internet or at the library.

First: Read the following story, "Fig and Molly." Students will wear white gloves and will use one gloved hand to act out *Fig's* character in the story and one gloved hand to act out *Molly's* character in the story.

Fig and Molly

In a small deep hole in the backyard of a 10-year-old boy named John Robert Daniels, there lived two field mice, *Fig* and *Molly. Fig* loved to scamper as fast as he could up and down the sides of the small deep hole. When he tired of that, he would scamper up and down the sides of another hole that was nearby. He could do it for hours, first one hole and then another. *Molly,* on the other hand, loved to stay at the bottom of the hole that was their home and cook seed pies. She would take the seeds that *Fig* had found for her, wash them very carefully, and place them in nice little rows on a wet leaf.

Of course *Molly* needed an oven in which to cook the seed pies, so *Fig* would run to the top of the hole, peer out to see if it was safe, and then dart along the edge of the fence until he found four small stones that had been made warm by the sun. He used the four stones to make an oven for *Molly.* Most of the time, it would take him four trips to bring the stones back into the hole. But it did not matter. He would make a hundred trips if he had to. *Fig* loved to eat seed pies more than anything else in the world.

One day as *Molly* prepared to bake a seed pie for *Fig's* birthday while *Fig* took a much-needed rest from scampering up and down the small deep holes, they both heard a strange sound that grew louder and louder. *Fig* and *Molly* became very frightened and held onto each other very tightly. All of a sudden a giant gush of water came roaring into the hole, spinning *Fig* and *Molly* in different directions. The little hole filled with water so quickly that *Fig* had no time to grab *Molly.* He clung to a small twig that stuck out of the side of the hole and held on as securely as he could, all the while looking for *Molly* and shouting her name. But he could not see where she had vanished.

Slowly, *Fig* climbed upward toward the opening of the hole. Holding on with all his might, he finally reached the top. And there, lying close to the hole, was the culprit: a long, green water hose, pouring so much water in and around the hole that *Fig* had to jump on top of the hose to keep him from being completely swept away.

Fig was sad. He wept and wept and called out for *Molly.* But no sound came from deep within the hole that had once been home to the two field mice. *Fig* kept crying and the water kept gushing. This was the worst day of his life.

As *Fig* began to dry his eyes and figure out how to get off the water hose, he turned around and looked toward his lost home one more time. Suddenly, floating up from the nearby hole that was rapidly filling up with water as well, came *Molly,* sitting in the middle of a beautiful wet leaf, holding a seed pie.

Fig jumped for joy and *Molly* hugged him very hard. And they both sat in the middle of John Robert Daniel's backyard and celebrated life by eating the entire seed pie, one seed at a time.

Next: Students will create a character development chart on the board by listing the different characteristics found in both characters. Students will share their own method of using their hands to show the characteristics of the two characters.

Then: Using those listed characteristics, students will draw their version of John Robert Daniel's backyard, or the inside of the field mice's hole, or an original ending to the story.

Finally: Students will think of other endings to the story and write those endings, and the teacher will read the story as the students act out the story and the new endings. Students will retell the story again, this time by becoming the characters rather than by simply using hands to create the characters. Children writing their own dialogue to the story rather than the teacher reading the story can enrich this retelling.

Alternative Assessment: Ask children to reflect, either by speaking, writing, or drawing, on this question, "What would you do to celebrate Molly's return?"

Activity 3

Content: Social Studies

Lesson: Hand Masks

Standard: Students will explore diversity in one's school and community and the benefits and challenges of a diverse population.

Multiple Intelligences: Bodily/Kinesthetic: Students will create adhesive masks using hands as molds. Intrapersonal: Students will use completed hand masks to answer reflective questions about diversity.

Materials: Fast-drying adhesive bandages, petroleum jelly, paper cups, black and white tempera paint, paintbrushes

Grade Level: 3–4

Objective: Students will create adhesive bandaging hand masks and use those masks as focal points for discussing issues of diversity.

Before: Use a student to model the appropriate method of creating an adhesive bandaging mask on a hand. Before the application begins, have students cut adhesive bandaging rolls, which can be purchased at medical supply stores, into ½-inch strips. The instructions are as follows:

a. Student will cover one hand in petroleum jelly.
b. A partner will apply adhesive strips on one side of the hand, either palm up or palm down. Each strip must be dipped in water and gently squeezed to remove the extra water.

c. Strips should be applied in a criss-cross position to ensure strength.

d. At least three layers of strips should be applied to each hand. Be extra careful between fingers. Apply extra strips in those areas to ensure strength.

e. When the last strip applied has dried, wait another two or three minutes before carefully prying off the adhesive mold from the hand.

f. Once mold has dried partially, apply either a design including white or black or a combination of both colors of tempera.

g. Let dry.

h. Place the completed hand masks on a long piece of white and black butcher paper.

First: Students will partner up and apply hand masks on each other. Parents or aides may assist in this experience. Each child will need to wear an old T-shirt and bring an old towel to class to use as a cushion for the hand when the adhesive bandaging is being applied. Students will paint and design their own hand masks.

Next: Place all of the hands on butcher paper that covers a long table. Have students stand around the table. Lead a discussion on the diversity of hand designs and shapes that have been created, and their connections to diversity and the way people in the room and elsewhere are different.

Then: Select one hand and ask this reflective question, "If this hand could speak, what would it say?" Choose another hand and this time ask a more pointed question such as, "If this hand could speak, what would it say about being different?" The students will then select different adhesive hands to use as stimuli for completing the following prompter phrases regarding diversity issues. Be sure to remind students to use answers appropriate to diversity, differences, tolerance, and so on.

a. "I wonder..."

b. "Time..."

c. "What is the first step in ..."

d. "I believe that..."

e. "How strange to..."

f. "Open your eyes and ..."

g. "Whenever I..."

h. "Suppose..."

i. "On one hand..."

j. "I try to..."

k. "How else do I know..."

l. "It takes..."

m. "Sometimes I forget to..."

n. "I make a difference when..."

o. "If I look long enough..."

Finally: Choose three varied age-appropriate articles from the newspaper. Discuss the articles. Ask the students this question: "If these hands could say something about these three situations, what would they say?"

Alternative Assessment: Allow students to use the hands as stimuli for any kind of classroom discussion.

Activity 4

Content: Social Studies

Lesson: Citizenship Cartoons

Standard: Students will describe the elements of fair play, good sportsmanship, and the idea of treating others the way they wish to be treated.

Multiple Intelligences: Visual/Spatial: Students will draw cartoon cells. Verbal/Linguistic: Students will write texts to accompany cartoon cells.

Materials: Art paper, crayons, rulers, hand masks

Grade Level: 3–4

Objective: Students will create eight-celled comic or cartoon strips about good citizenship, using *hands* as the central characters. Students will exchange strips and then write an original story line to accompany the cartoon strip they have been given.

Before: Lead a discussion on good citizenship and fair play. Suggested questions might include:

    a. What is good citizenship?

    b. When did you exhibit good citizenship during the past few days? Today?

    c. Name one thing that doesn't seem quite fair to you.

    d. How would you handle the following scenarios or problems?

        1. Someone cuts in line on the way to lunch.

        2. Someone older than you is having trouble opening a door.

        3. You get called out at first base during a softball game on the playground.

        4. You are too tired to set the table for dinner.

        5. You argue with your older or younger brother or sister about toys, taking the trash out, where to sit in the car, and so on.

First: Students will use art paper, rulers, and markers to create an eight-celled cartoon strip including space below each cell for the addition of written text. Students will think of a story or idea they can draw in those eight cells, which have to do with good citizenship, fair play, or being treated equally. Remind students that the main character must be a pair of hands instead of a human.

Next: When cells are completed, students will take someone else's cell and, using that cartoon as a stimulus, write an original story that applies to good citizenship, fair play, or being treated equally.

Then: Students will read the stories aloud to the class and discuss personal connections to the stories.

Finally: Students and teacher will create a one-line class rule that applies to good citizenship.

Alternative Assessment: Draw a picture of what fair play looks like.

Activity 5

Content: Language Arts

Lesson: Creative Writing

Standard: Use the writing process, including generating topics, drafting, revising ideas, and editing, to complete effectively a variety of writing tasks.

Multiple Intelligence: Verbal/Linguistic: Students will complete a variety of writing tasks.

Materials: A collection of completed hand masks

Grade Level: 3–4

Objective: The students will use the collection of hand masks as stimuli for a variety of writing tasks.

Before: Have students stand around the table of hand masks. Students will generate topics, which come from observing the hands. Some topics or ideas might include:

    a. A day in the life of . . .

    b. Point of view of . . .

    c. The mystery of . . .

    d. My own hand . . .

    e. The collection of hands . . .

    f. Occupations

    g. Poetry

    h. Puppetry skit

First: Students will use the writing process of drafting, revising, and editing to create a writing piece, which connects to one of or a collection of the hand masks.

Next: Students will create an exhibit of writing pieces and hand masks. They will write and send invitations to other classes to view the exhibit.

Then: Students from other classes will choose a writing piece they have read or a hand mask they have seen and use those as their own stimuli for creating an appropriate art piece, either clay or drawing or free-form newspaper sculpture.

Finally: Students who have written the hand pieces will reflect, either orally or in writing, on this question, "Hands are like words when . . . "

Alternative Assessment: Use a variety of magazine pictures that show different hands. Have children talk about what the hands in the pictures are saying.

Activity 6

Content: Social Studies, Language Arts

Lesson: Biographies

Standard: Students will use stories to describe past events, people, and places with emphasis on daily life in past time and different places.

Multiple Intelligences: Bodily/Kinesthetic: Students will create adhesive hand masks. Verbal/Linguistic: Students will write a biography. Visual/Spatial: Students will draw and design a community mural.

Materials: Hand masks, art supplies, butcher paper

Grade Level: 3–4

Objective: Students will research various roles that men, women, and children played in the daily life of a wagon train. Students will select one role (wagon master, scout, cook, horse wrangler, cattle drover, child, mother, father, and so on) and create a hand mask that defines that role. Students will write an original biography of that person's life and responsibilities as a member of a wagon train.

Before: Show several movie clips of the daily life on a wagon train. A list of these old movies can be found online at http://www.fiftiesweb.com/wt/wagon-train.htm. Students will discuss the different roles that were observed in the clips, and the hardships and dangers that were apparent to the various members of the wagon train.

First: Select one member of the wagon train on which to gather research. Use the writing process to complete a finished piece of writing that is biographical in nature. The writing can be original in its story line.

Next: Use the writing as a stimulus for creating a hand mask, which shows, through its shape and form, a task that is being done by that particular wagon train member that requires the use of hands. For example, a cook's hands may show the cook holding a knife with which to cut potatoes or holding a spoon with which to stir a pot of soup. The student forms his or her hand into that shape, and another student creates a hand mask of that particular hand shape.

Then: Students make comparisons through drawings, Venn diagrams, or charts of the role technology has played in changing the way similar tasks are accomplished now as opposed to the way they were in historical times.

Finally: Students will write a first-person point of view journal entry of their characters or a reflective paragraph of the process of creating the hand mask to fit the character's task.

Alternative Assessment: Create a mural depicting the daily life tasks accomplished by the various wagon train characters that the students researched.

Activity 7

Content: Social Studies, Math

Lesson: Interviewing Skills

Standard: Use resource materials and interviews to trace the history of your family.

Multiple Intelligences: Interpersonal: Students will interview members of their immediate family. Logical/Mathematical: Students will create a comparison chart.

Materials: Sample questionnaires

Grade Level: 1–3

Objective: Students will construct an interview questionnaire relating to jobs people do. Students will administer the questionnaire to family members. Students will create a comparison chart of the information gathered.

Before: Show several samples of questionnaires. These can be found in newspapers, in magazines, on the Internet, and so on. Children will discuss the qualities of a good questionnaire.

First: Students will brainstorm, in groups, questions they might ask family members about jobs they do.

Next: Students will narrow the list of questions and select five questions. The students will then create a questionnaire format and use the computer to type it up and make copies. Some suggested questionnaire questions may include:

   a. Describe three different jobs you have held in which you had to use your hands to accomplish the task required of the job.

   b. What was the hardest job you ever had?

   c. Tell me why your hands are important in your job.

   d. Is there a technology tool that can do your job better than you? What is it?

   e. Why are your thumbs important in your ability to do your job?

Then: Students will share their questionnaire answers with the class. Students will make some inferences from the collection of answers.

Finally: Complete this reflective question, either by discussing or writing, "Three things I cannot do without thumbs are _____, _____, and _____. Three things I can do without thumbs are _____, _____, and _____."

Alternative Assessment: Research three members of the animal kingdom. Show through art, discussion, or writing how they survive with or without thumbs.

❘ *And now, what about five good lessons from one good book?* See if these work.

The book: Anderson, Ruth. (2002). *Cinderella.* Boston: Little, Brown and Company.

   a. Read page 10 of this wonderfully illustrated and freshly interpreted version of an old, old story. Look closely at the illustrations. Here is a bit of math for the students to do:

   1. Give students a pile of dried lentils.

   2. Students will count the dried lentils.

3. Students will multiply the lentils according to the number of thumbs found in the illustrations on page 10.

4. Students will put dried lentils into piles according to the number of all the pinkies found on page 10.

5. Students will make up one math-counting problem using the dried lentils and the illustration found on page 10.

b. Read the book, *Cinderella*, and make a list of all the chores Cinderella had to do: laundry, weed, cook, sew, fix hair, fetch a fan, and so on. Students will act out those chores nonverbally and verbally as well.

c. Use the illustrations of the book to discover what functions required the use of hands. Students will think of verbs that connect to each function. Here are some suggested function connections:

1. broom—sweep
2. pail—pour
3. spade—dig
4. mirror—look
5. bowl—hold
6. wand—wave
7. fan—flutter

d. Students will read the story again and look at the illustrations. They will discuss the tasks Cinderella had to undertake that required the use of both hands.

e. Students will find small sticks. They will sand, paint, and add glitter to these sticks to create their own magic wands. Students may wish to call these sticks their *Good Deed Magic Wands*. The boys and girls will keep track of all the times they use their magic wands during the course of the school day. At the end of the day, the class will share the good deeds with each other. They may even wish to create their own Cinderella class booklet, compiling drawings and writings about certain good deeds.

✔ *Oh yes. Remember the teachable moment* that introduced our activities in this chapter? Well, here is a little lesson to go with that idea.

Activity 8

Content: Social Studies, Math

Lesson: Comparisons

Standard: Students will find physical similarities in family members.

Multiple Intelligences: Visual/Spatial and Logical/Mathematical: Students will observe the hands of family members for similar physical characteristics. Students will draw those similarities. Students will draw conclusions.

Materials: Art paper

Grade Level: 1–3

Objective: Students will observe the hands of family members for evidence of similar physical characteristics. Students will make comparisons between the physical characteristics of their own hands and those of their family members.

Before: Teacher will read the scenario that begins this chapter. Students will then show their hands to other members of the class and make distinctions among them. Teacher will lead a discussion on the differences that are observed.

First: Students will create a drawing of their own hands and label the interesting physical characteristics such as scars, freckles, finger length, fingernails, and so on. All the drawings will be placed on a table. Students must look at the drawings and match them to their rightful owners.

Next: Students will select several family members and create a drawing of their hands as well, labeling the interesting physical characteristics that are observed.

Then: Students will bring the labeled drawings to class and make presentations of their findings.

Finally: Students will draw conclusions about the physical similarities found in their drawings and what their hands may look like as they get older.

Alternative Assessment: Research the similarities and differences in paw prints of wild animals.

And finally, if you think *a picture is worth a thousand words,* use the drawing of *Hands* below to engage your students in seeing, writing, drawing, or just thinking about hands, or feet, or noses, or ears, or chins, for that matter, in a different and more interesting way. The next activities will work wonders for boys and girls who must see it in order to get it.

Activity 9

Content: Physical Activity

Lesson: Tossing and Catching Objects

Standard: Students will demonstrate progress toward the mature form of selected manipulative, locomotor, and nonlocomotor skills.

Multiple Intelligence: Bodily/Kinesthetic: Students will use their bodies to throw, catch, and roll objects.

Materials: Various size rubber balls

Grade Level: K

Objective: Students will practice rolling, tossing, and catching rubber balls and bean bags of varying sizes.

Before: Look at the hands drawing on the previous page. Ask any older student who knows how to juggle to come into the room and show the younger boys and girls this physical activity.

First: Lead a discussion of why juggling is an almost impossible task to accomplish and what practice needs to happen first.

Next: Sit children on the floor in a circle. Use a large ball to roll to someone in the circle. That person will roll the large ball to another person, and so on. Do this activity with different size balls.

Then: In pairs, students will roll various size balls to each other. They will then toss various smaller balls to each other.

Finally: Students will reflect upon the difficulty of tossing and catching and will think of suggestions that might make tossing and catching easier. If possible, locate a video of someone juggling. Show this to the children.

Alternative Assessment: Create a classroom obstacle course that includes degrees of difficulty in rolling, tossing, or catching balls.

Activity 10

Content: Language Arts

Lesson: Rhythmic Poem

Standard: Students will echo short rhythms and patterns.

Multiple Intelligences: Bodily/Kinesthetic: Students will use hands to clap a steady beat. Verbal/Linguistic: Students will learn a poem.

Materials: None

Grade Level: K–3

Objective: Students will recite a poem with rhythmic hand beats.

Before: Teach the class the old rhythmic chant, "The Minister's Cat," which includes clapping the hands four beats at the end of each line. Students will say the following line and add an adjective to the line that begins with consecutive letters of the alphabet. After each line, they will clap four times.

> The minister's cat is an *angry* cat. (clap, clap, clap, clap)
> The minister's cat is a *bashful* cat. (clap, clap, clap, clap)
> The minister's cat is a *cute* cat. (clap, clap, clap, clap)

Students will continue this repetitive line all the way through the alphabet or as long as they can think of different adjectives.

First: Sit in a circle. Choose a student whose name begins with the letter *A*. Students will describe this particular student with an adjective that begins with the letter *A*. Put that person's name and his or her descriptive adjective on a white board or chart paper so that the class can read it. Continue with another student whose name begins with the letter *B*. Do likewise with that student, having the rest of the class find a descriptive word beginning with the letter *B* that fits that particular student, and so on. Place each person's name and descriptive word on the board. Do about one third of the class at a time.

Next: Students will say the newly created chant, clapping four times at the end of each line or phrase.

Then: Students will get into groups and create their own rhythmic chants using vocabulary words from curricular areas being studied, names of sports figures, toys, weather, native tribe names, or any topic that is of interest to them.

Finally: Students will look at the drawing of the clapping hand again and create an original rhythmic pattern of hand claps.

Alternative Assessment: Students will write a rhythmic chant using names of family members.

Activity 11

Content: Comprehensive Health

Lesson: Verbal and Nonverbal Communication

Standard: Students will distinguish between verbal and nonverbal communication.

Multiple Intelligence: Bodily/Kinesthetic: Students will use nonverbal body clues for communication. Students will learn sign language.

Materials: None

Grade Level: 2–3

Objective: Students will demonstrate an understanding of different forms of communication: verbal, nonverbal, and sign language.

Before: Call out the following words or phrases, or call out words or phrases similar to these. Students will give different verbal responses that mean the same as the words or phrases.

Hello.	Are you sure?	Bye!
Yes.	You!	It's cold.
No.	What time is it?	It's hot.
What?	Slow down!	I'm hungry.

First: Students will listen to the words and phrases again. They will give different nonverbal or body responses that mean the same as the words or phrases.

Next: Lead students in a discussion about verbal and nonverbal communication. Students will create nonverbal scenarios such as these below. Other class members will explain the scenarios in verbal terms.

Feeding the pet dog his breakfast

Opening a book and reading outloud

Diving into water

Walking into a Halloween haunted house

Going through the cafeteria line at school

Then: Teach students how to communicate through sign language. Use the drawing of hands to show how to say the word "hand."

Finally: Students will learn how to sign their own name.

Alternative Assessment: Give classroom directions at least once every day in sign language.

Activity 12

Content: Language Arts

Lesson: Telling Stories

Standard: Students will use effective vocabulary and organization to relate information.

Multiple Intelligences: Visual/Spatial: Students will use the hands drawing as a stimulus for telling a story. Verbal/Linguistic: Students will tell a story. Intrapersonal: Students will reflect upon past experiences.

Materials: Copies of the hands drawing

Grade Level: K–3

Objective: Students will look at the different elements of the drawing in this chapter and tell an original story.

Before: Students will review important aspects of telling a story.

First: Students will use the hands drawing as a stimulus for telling stories about different experiences happening in the scenes in the picture.

Next: Students will relate personal stories that correspond to the original stories being told.

Then: Students will answer "What would happen if…" questions about the picture.

Finally: Students will reflect upon their own appreciation of the drawing.

Alternative Assessment: Students will take a drawing home and ask a family member to tell them a story that comes from viewing the drawing.

To wrap up this chapter, here is every idea you ever wanted to know about hands. Hand these over to your students and see what happens.

Hands K–3

V/L	Write a creative story about what one hand can do.	Read children's books such as Audrey Wood's *Piggies*.	Write your own story about your hands in the format of Wood's book.	Use newspaper photos to lead discussions on different uses of hands.	Create language arts activities using "hand mask" as the stimulus.
L/M	From this kind of collection, compare the way hands are drawn and/or used.	Use groups of hands in the class to create problem-solving scenarios.	Create problem-solving scenarios using single hand masks as a stimulus.	Create comparison charts about occupations and hands.	Compare a human hand to various animal hands.
V/S	Draw an eight-celled comic about hands.	Look at pictures of the anatomy of a hand.	Design a mechanical hand.	Draw your own hand(s) doing the thing it likes to do best.	Create hand collages from magazine pictures.
B/K	Use fast-drying adhesive bandaging to create a hand sculpture.	With your own hands, duplicate the hand formations found in the book.	Learn the American Sign Language alphabet.	Create hand or finger puppets in connection with a report.	Use hands to define different emotions.
M/R	Engage in call/response rhythms using hand beats.	Listen to hand percussion music. Discuss.	Create hand ostinatos using your first and/or last names.	Listen to various musical instruments. Discuss the relationship of hands to making music.	Sing along to well-known melodies. Practice keeping the beat with your hands.
Inter	Teach it to your parents or siblings.	Write the text for someone else's comic strip.	Give a joint report on hands and technology.	Create a symbolic hand. Share with the class.	Interview your parents regarding using hands in their work and around the house.
Intra	Draw one of your hands. Label what each part of your hand does for you.	Write a first-person poem about your hand.	"The one thing I would miss most about not having hands would be _____."	"I use my hands and feet equally when I _____."	Use as a reflective journal stimulus.
N	Humans. Insects. Animals. Report on hands at work. Write about or discuss.	Take a trip around the school. Discuss evidence of hands at work.	Research areas of technology where hands are obsolete.	Follow your hands and their connection to the environment.	Tell that story in some form.

The activities and experiences in this grid are just a bit more difficult and can bring some challenges to your students. These ideas can be used as extension lessons or individual projects, or in some cases, centers.

Hands 4–6

V/L	Write a story using two drawings from the art pictorial book in the "Dear Teacher" letter.	Discuss similes, metaphors, and so on that use the word "hands."	Write the directions on how a thumb works.	Write an expository essay about hands and certain occupations.	Write that story from a hand's point of view.
L/M	Compare ways different illustrators draw hands for children's books.	Create a chart of how often different fingers are used in a given time.	Create comparison charts regarding white-collar and blue-collar jobs.	Chart the way a pet uses his paws. Make a concluding statement.	Sequence actions of picking up a pencil with no hands.
V/S	Draw illustrations for the directions.	Look at pictures of the anatomy of a hand.	Design and label a mechanical hand for a specific job.	Draw your own hand. Label its distinctions.	Using imagery, lead the class on a journey that a hand might take.
B/K	Create a group sculpture with completed adhesive hands. Place in library.	Create a movement piece from each sculpture.	Construct the hand from various materials such as paper rolls, wire, and so on.	View a Marcel Marceau video. Practice pantomime moves performed by Mr. Marceau.	Engage in an experiment of doing daily classroom tasks with no hands.
M/R	Pick three musical instruments. Listen to music. Discuss how hands play a role in musical distinctions.	Visit a high school band practice. Listen for differences in sounds and hand dexterities.	Create a rap, chant, or song about these two lists of bones.	Create certain pantomime movements to music. Use music as the catalyst.	Practice hand functions used in playing different sports.
Inter	Teach a lesson on the importance of thumbs.	Interview staff and faculty at school. Ask this question: "How do hands contribute to the success of your job?"	Present that report to the class.	Interview a mechanic and a surgeon. Present an oral report on similarities involving how both use hands.	Lead an experiment of different handshakes. Research and present a report to class.
Intra	Reflect upon expressions such as "hands on," "hands down," and so on.	Write a short biography of one of your fingers.	Have your palm read. Reflect upon its meaning.	Keep a journal entry of this experience.	Write your own definition of "blue collar" and "white collar."
N	Students will "give up" one part of their body (hand, legs, eyes, etc.) for an hour. Discuss.	Research animals and how aspects of their adaptability depend upon their paws, hooves, and so on.	Learn the bones of the human hand and bones of one animal's paw. Compare.	Study areas of medical research whereby mechanical hands are used for safety reasons.	Research biohazard gear.

MACHINES

Dear Teacher,

Ask a student to explain how a stapler works. Ask a group of six children to use their bodies to model how a manual pencil sharpener operates. Play "I Spy" with simple machines found in the room as the category. Debate the most important machine created in this or the last century. Ask a first grader how the human body works. These are some starter ideas to use when beginning a unit or lesson on machines, ideas that offer an open entry into the subject, a way for kids to use discovery techniques initially before they fill in the blanks and their minds with facts and information.

In my last book, *Dancing Hearts* (Golden, CO: Fulcrum Publishing, 1997), I devoted one chapter to Judy Barrett's wonderful children's classic, *Cloudy with a Chance of Meatballs* (New York: Atheneum, 1978). Using that particular book as a catalyst and an idea from the *Dancing Hearts* book to whet their educational appetites, my university students engaged in an activity that required them to put together parts from old appliances and create original "machines" that could be used to solve some of the weather-related problems found in *Cloudy with a Chance of Meatballs*. Once the original machines were completed, the university students created a hands-on Junk Machine Museum for the elementary students in the schools we served. We included "What if . . . " questions about the machines. We asked the elementary students to draw additional parts of the machines to improve their functions. We asked them to use the machines as stimuli for creative writing endeavors. We offered open-ended questions, which required them to use the illustrations of Barrett's book to help answer the questions. We asked them to think of logical names for the machines. And we asked them to solve the weather-related problems discussed in the book by designing and drawing up original blueprints of their own that would solve a specific situation.

Soon the whole blueprint idea mushroomed into other experiences. We took the original blueprints and gave them to another class, who tried to "read" the blueprints and build the machines accordingly, using materials such as string, toothpicks, paper plates and cups, and toilet paper rolls rather than actual appliance parts. Then, those students who constructed the machines from the blueprints were asked to write directions on how to construct the machines. Those written directions were given to yet another class, who tried to construct the machines using that method.

All in all, children had an opportunity to use several intelligences to help make meaning of something: visual/spatial intelligence for looking at drawings, verbal/linguistic intelligence for writing directions for constructing the machines, and logical/mathematical intelligence for making sense of the sequentially written directions for constructing the machines. In these efforts, the children also were able to use their bodily/kinesthetic capacities to actually build the machines.

To get this particular chapter off to an interesting start, here is something you may wish to do with your boys and girls. First, place two cardboard boxes of different sizes next to each other. Then ask the students, in pairs, to use any object or objects they can find in the room to help them move a pencil or book from the lower cardboard box to the taller one. Once each experiment has finished, discuss the functions of the simple machines they created to complete the task at hand and what sequence of events they used to complete the task, and then spend some time brainstorming existing machines that use the same function or method of completing a similar task.

You will also find in this chapter several activities, experiences, and even a children's musical that focuses on the concept of work itself. In other words, machines are not the answer to the myriad situations that come our way on a daily basis. Rather, the complex ideas of work, work ethics, the life skill of perseverance, and our own relationships to things that make our lives easier are elements in a child's life that are important enough to give space to at this particular time in the chapter on machines.

Your favorite watch is not working and you know it isn't the battery. So you shake it violently, but that doesn't do the trick. Then you remember how, when you were a child, you would watch your younger brother get your mother's old watch, take it all apart, and put it back together again without one piece left over. And get it to work. "I think I can do this," you say, as you look for something to pry off the back of the watch.

A couple of hours go by and you marvel at how many pieces of watch have accumulated on the kitchen table. By midafternoon, you begin to wonder if your brother is still on that cruise to Alaska and if they might have ship-to-shore phone service.

At 6 o'clock, your life begins to pass before your very eyes, so you go next door and grab the 5-year-old neighbor boy and plop him down at the kitchen table while you start dinner. You watch him put the watch together in less time than it takes to find the Shake 'n' Bake in the back of the pantry, and in an instant, you have the makings of a brilliant lesson on machines. A teachable moment has ticked into your life, and you are ever so pleased.

Activity 1

Content: Language Arts

Lesson: Poetry

Standard: Students will write an original poem.

Multiple Intelligences: Verbal/Linguistic: Students will write a poem. Visual/Spatial: Students will observe parts of a pencil sharpener to aid them in the writing of a poem.

Materials: Pencil sharpener

Grade Level: 3

Objective: Students will disassemble a manual pencil sharpener and write a poem about its pieces.

Before: Students will find an old manual pencil sharpener and take it apart.

First: Students will discuss the various pieces of the pencil sharpener, their functions, and how they relate to and work with the other parts of the sharpener in order for the entire machine to function.

Next: Students will select one piece of the pencil sharpener and write a poem about it.

Then: Students will read poems aloud to each other.

Finally: Students will use the piece of sharpener used for the poetry writing as a means of comparing it and its function to three other machines and similar pieces and functions.

Alternative Assessment: Students will show how to put the sharpener back together again. They will write a poem about a whole pencil sharpener.

Activity 2

Content: Science

Lesson: Building Machines with Clay

Standard: Students will construct models that illustrate simple concepts and compare them to what they represent.

Multiple Intelligences: Logical/Mathematical: Students will make comparisons. Bodily/Kinesthetic: Students will construct machines out of clay. Verbal/Linguistic: Students will discuss various aspects of selected machines. Intrapersonal: Students will write a journal entry comparing themselves to certain machines.

Materials: Magazines, clay

Grade Level: 3

Objective: Students will discuss machines found in the home or at school that make their lives easier or more difficult. Students will create one of those machines from clay. Students will find an authentic picture of the machine that they created in clay. Students will compare the two.

Before: Students will cut out pictures of machines from magazines that can be found in the home or at school.

First: Students will have a discussion about how certain machines make their lives easier or more difficult. Students will use the magazine pictures as catalysts for the discussion.

Next: Students will create a selected machine out of clay.

Then: Students will discuss how the clay machines work and how they are alike or different from the machines they chose from the magazines.

Finally: Students will either draw or write a journal entry answering the reflective statement: "I am most like a _____ machine when I _____."

Alternative Assessment: Students will write one fact card about one machine and collate all of the cards into a collection of facts about machines, which can be placed in a container for future use.

Activity 3

Content: Science

Lesson: Constructing a Pencil Sharpener

Standard: Students will construct models that illustrate simple concepts and compare them to what they represent.

Multiple Intelligences: Bodily/Kinesthetic: Students will build a model of a machine. Visual/Spatial: Students will draw designs. Verbal/Linguistic: Students will read and follow directions.

Materials: Paper rolls, string, cardboard, and so on

Grade Level: 3

Objective: Students will construct an original machine that can sharpen pencils and demonstrate its function.

Before: Students will discuss how manual and electric pencil sharpeners work.

First: Students will use various materials and supplies to design, label, and construct a machine that sharpens pencils in a different way.

Next: Students will draw the new designs and label the parts.

Then: Students will select other students' labeled designs to be used as blueprints for constructing someone else's original machines.

Finally: Students will display the new machines and discuss the ease or difficulty in following someone else's directions.

Alternative Assessment: Students will write an ad for their new pencil sharpener.

Activity 4

Content: Life Skills

Lesson: Children's Musical

Standards: Students will demonstrate an understanding of teamwork skills, recognize and participate in leadership roles, and understand dependability, trustworthiness, productivity, and initiative. Students will use reading comprehension strategies.

Multiple Intelligences: All: Students will use various workplace skills and intelligences to successfully present and perform in a children's musical about perseverance and work ethic.

Materials: Appropriate materials, sheet music, supplies for the play

Grade Level: 3 combined with 4–6

Objective: Students will participate in the play, *The Flea Who Could Sing, Dance, and Play Chopsticks*, as a vehicle for demonstrating specific life, workplace, and academic skills.

Before: Students will spend time familiarizing themselves with certain life skills and will demonstrate an understanding of these life skill definitions and specific instances in which these life skills are used in their daily lives, at home, and at school.

First: Students will, as a self-contained class or with assistance from a fourth-, fifth-, or sixth-grade class, rehearse and present the following children's musical, *The Flea Who Could Sing, Dance, and Play Chopsticks*, attending specifically to the various life, workplace, and academic skills of perseverance, teamwork, effort, tolerance, critical thinking, problem solving, leadership, communication, dependability, initiative, technology, goal setting, follow-through, decision making, reading, and writing afforded them during this experience.

The Flea Who Could Sing, Dance, and Play Chopsticks

Words and Music by Martha Brady

Scene 1: Classroom

Students enter from all areas of the audience onto the stage. Students will be carrying books, coats, lunch sacks, basketballs, and so on. Students will *ad-lib* as they prepare for the bell to ring and for class to begin. Teacher is writing on the board, oblivious of the children.

[Sound effect: Ticking of clock and buzzer.]

[NARRATOR is stage right, sitting on a stool.]

[If a girl plays the main character, the character's name is Tessa Alexandria Humple. If a boy plays the main character, the character's name is Troy Alexander Humple.]

Narrator: This is the story of Troy. Troy Humple, to be exact. Troy Alexander Humple, to be really exact. Troy Alexander Humple III, if you want to be totally correct and really exact. And we want to be totally correct and really exact about this. Troy Alexander Humple III is in the third grade at _____ School. He looks like almost every other 8-year-old boy in Mrs. Thompson's third-grade class at _____ School. He has sandy hair, a few freckles floating across his nose, and a missing tooth from the time he fell off his grandmother's roof. He wears long, baggy shorts almost all of the time, and Nikes that are too big for him. He even has a scar on his face from the time Lawrence Foley accidentally thought Troy's head was a baseball and accidentally hit him square between the eyes with a twenty-ounce bat. Yes, Troy Alexander Humple III is like every other 8-year-old boy in Mrs. Thompson's third-grade class at _____ School. Well, almost.

[Buzzer goes off and children settle down and face MRS. THOMPSON. Enter TROY, whose arms are loaded with books, coats, lunch, and so on. He walks toward a seat, spilling his armload of "stuff," knocking things off desks, and in general making a real mess of the room.]

Narrator: See what I mean? Wait! There's more.

Mrs. Thompson: Boys and girls, may I have your attention? We need to attend to our morning duties before we begin class. So [looks around], who are my helpers this morning?

Rachel: I'm the blackboard cleaner, Mrs. Thompson. [RACHEL rises and "cleans" the blackboard.]

Trish: I empty the trash, Mrs. Thompson. [TRISH rises and takes the trash out to empty, then returns.]

Marta: I sharpen the pencils, Mrs. Thompson. [MARTA collects pencils from MRS. THOMPSON'S desk and sharpens them.]

James: I'm in charge of lunch count, Mrs. Thompson. [Students raise their hands and JAMES counts outloud.]

Ryan: I count the labels, Mrs. Thompson. [RYAN goes back to a spot on stage and begins to count coupons.]

Mrs. Thompson: Excellent, Ryan. How many have we collected so far?

Ryan: 739,452 . . . and a half. [Holds up a torn coupon.]

Mrs. Thompson: That's marvelous, class, now only 544,681 more cream of mushroom soup can labels and we can get a brand new electric pencil sharpener for the room. Isn't this exciting? [ALL ad-lib excitement.] Now, have all my helpers completed their tasks? [Looks at TROY.] Troy, aren't you in charge of watering the plants this week? [TROY rises and grabs a water container from the teacher's desk as she continues to talk. He walks over to a "plant" at the edge of the stage, stumbles, and tosses "water" (confetti) out into the audience as MRS. THOMPSON continues her lines.] Okay, class, now while Troy is watering the plant the rest of us will prepare ourselves for our lessons. So what is the distance betwe_____ [MRS. THOMPSON sees TROY'S goof.]. . . . Troy, you may *sit down* now.

Narrator: See what I mean?

Mrs. Thompson: *As I was saying*, it is time for us to begin class, so boys and girls, what is the first thing we do each and every morning?

All: The Pledge of Allegiance!!! [TROY begins saying the Pledge of Allegiance as the other children scowl at him.]

[Song: PLEDGE OF ALLEGIANCE] (Sheet music for all songs found at end of play.)

[At the end of the song, TROY concludes by saying . . . "with liberty and justice for all." MRS. THOMPSON claps and smiles.]

Mrs. Thompson [Giggly.]**:** I love it. . . . Wonderful, wonderful. I absolutely adore this class. It puts me in such a good mood almost every day. I don't care what the second-grade teachers say, this is a wonderful class. Where was I? Oh, yes. I have several announcements to make this morning and I think I'll begin with the one that will be most exciting for you. So, if I can have everyone's attention. [TROY straightens and immediately knows something off his desk.] Boys and girls, _____ School is going to have its very first All-School Pet Trick Show.

Narrator: An All-School Pet Trick Show?

Class: An All-School Pet Trick Show?

Narrator: That's what I said.

Mrs. Thompson: That's what I said. An All-School Pet Trick Show.

[ALL ad-lib excitement.]

Mrs. Thompson: We'll talk about it tomorrow, class, but now it is time for a story, so if you will come back to my rocking chair, I will read you a wonderful story about a pet boa constrictor and how he ate all the farmer's clothes on his clothesline. Then it will be time for recess.

[ALL but TROY go silently off stage while TROY works his way to the front of the stage.]

Troy: But I don't own a pet. I've never owned a pet. [TROY walks off stage, dejectedly.]

Narrator: It's true. Troy didn't own a pet. In fact, he had never owned a pet. In all of his almost nine years, there had never been a dog in his house, or a cat, or a hamster, or a mouse, or a bird, or even a fish. Not one pet. There had never even been a calendar hung up in his house with a picture of a pet on it. As Troy walks home, all he can think about is the All-School Pet Trick Show and the fact that he has no pet.

[TROY walks off.]

[UP MUSIC—set change to PLAYGROUND.]

[TROY walks onto the playground set. He meets several students who are talking about the pet trick show. TROY walks slowly and is very downcast and quiet.]

Debbie [To TROY]: This is going to be so cool, don't you think? Huh, Troy? What kind of pet do you have? And can it do a trick?

[TROY shrugs and looks down. DEBBIE walks on past.]

Bill: Hey, Troy, are you going to teach your dog a trick? You do have a dog, don't you?

Liz: Then maybe a cat? Do you have a cat, Troy?

Stephanie: No cat? Hm. How about a gerbil? Do you have a gerbil, Troy?

Julie: Goldfish? A teeny, weeny, tiny, itty, bitty goldfish?

[TROY continues to shrug and look downcast.]

Suzanne: Well, I have a pet parrot that can yell like Tarzan.

Sam: And I have a pet snake that can spell the word "Mississippi" with his body.

Trish: And I've got a dog that can do a school cheer.

[ALL of the students begin to ad-lib outlandish tricks their pets can do.]

Suzanne: If you ask me, all of our pets have to be really, really smart to be in this pet trick show. Really smart! Really, really smart!

[Song: SMART PETS]

[Sound effect: Bell rings]

Stephanie: That's the bell, everybody; school's out. I've got to get home now to start practicing pet tricks with my pet. Hey Troy, what is your pet's trick going to be?

Wayne: Yeah, Humple, what brilliant pet trick idea are *you* going to come up with?

Troy [Very quietly]: Oh, I don't know. Something . . . I guess.

Wayne: What did you say? I can't hear you.

Troy [a bit louder]: I said, I don't know. . . . Something.

Stephanie: Well, what kind of pet *do* you have?

Troy [softly]: I, er, I don't have a pet.

All: Huh?

Troy [louder]: I said, *I don't have a pet.*

[ALL look at each other and laugh, softly at first, then louder and louder as they exit, pointing at TROY.]

[TROY lowers his head and exits slowly.]

Narrator: That moment had to be the worst moment of Troy Alexander Humple's life. It had to be worse than the time he accidentally hit the button that dropped the automatic garage door onto the hood of his dad's brand-new Porsche. It had to be worse than the time his sister's boyfriend called and Troy had answered the phone and told him that his sister had become a nun. It was even worse than the day he got caught trying to raffle off his big brother at the mall one Christmas. Yes, this was the all-time worst moment in his life. So, with the worst moment of his life imprinted all over his body (TROY slumps even more so), Troy Alexander Humple walked on home.

[UP MUSIC—set change to LIVING ROOM.]

[Enter MOM, who dusts furniture, turns on the TV, and watches a soap opera.]

Troy [Enters]: Mom? I'm home.

Mom [Gets up and energetically dusts TROY.]: Oh, there you are, sweetie. [MOM kisses the top of TROY'S head and turns off the TV.] Did you have a good day at school? I saved four more cream of mushroom soup can labels for you, honey.

Troy: Thanks, Mom. Yeah, it was an okay day, I guess. Mrs. Thompson was in a good mood.

Mom: That's wonderful, Troy. I like it when Mrs. Thompson is in a good mood. It makes you in a better mood, too, when you get home every day. You know?

[MOM exits briefly.]

Troy: Mom, something came up at school today that I need to talk to you about. It has to do with a p _____ [looks and sees that MOM has left].

[Enter DAD with a newspaper. DAD goes immediately to the TV and turns it on.]

Dad: Clara, I'm home. What's for dinner? Oh, hi Troy. What's up? [Begins reading the newspaper.]

Troy: Dad, can I talk to you a minute about something that is happening at school? It has to do with a show about tricks . . . a p_____

[Enter MOM again.]

Mom [Interrupts TROY]: Hi, honey. Hard day? [MOM pats DAD'S head and accidentally picks up his toupee by mistake.] Oops, sorry. I always do that. [MOM begins to dust the top of DAD'S bald head.]

Dad [A bit unraveled]: Uh, that's okay. What did you say was for dinner? [DAD places his toupee back on his head.]

Mom: Why, cream of mushroom soup, of course.

Dad: I should have guessed.

[Enter BIG SIS, who blows in.]

Big Sis: Any calls? [Exits.] I'll be on the phone if you need me.

Troy: Mom, Dad, I'd like to talk to you about maybe getting a p_____

[Enter BIG BROTHER, combing his hair.]

Big Brother: Can I borrow the car for a sec, Dad? [Goes and picks up the car keys, and the two of them wrestle a bit.]

Troy: Mom, Dad, I was wondering if, er, uh, if, er, if I could possibly . . . get a pet?

[ALL stop and freeze. They stare at TROY, then at each other, then begin to laugh, softly at first, then louder and louder as they exit.]

[TROY is left in the room alone.]

Troy: I guess that was a no. [Begins to look around the room.] One pet. Just one pet. That is all I have ever wanted. Just one. That is all I've ever dreamed of.

[Song: WHEN YOU HAVE A DREAM]

[This song can be sung by TROY onstage, or it can be sung by another student using a microphone offstage. While the song is being sung, a "dream sequence" dance or movement activity by other students can be performed on stage.]

[TROY stays on stage while NARRATOR speaks.]

Narrator: On the next day, which was Saturday, Troy didn't have to ask his mom and dad the question again. He knew the answer. There was definitely no room in their home for a pet, any kind of pet. So he began to do some heavy-duty thinking.

Troy: I know. I'll borrow a pet. Just for a week or two. Just long enough to teach him a trick. Then I'll return him. No one will have to know. I'll teach him tricks in the back yard or in the lot across the street. That will work. I know that will work. Now, let's see, where would I find a pet that would like to be borrowed? [Thinks long and hard.] *The zoo!* [Troy exits.]

[UP MUSIC—set change to THE ZOO.]

[Sound effects: Zoo animal noises]

[Enter ZOO ANIMALS that are in "cages" and nerdy ZOO VISITORS who ad-lib watching the animals. Nerds sit on a bench before TROY enters.]

Narrator: For the first time that day, Troy began to feel a smile work its way up his face. By the time he got to the zoo, he was covered with grins and a few tickles. He walked among the cages to get a sense of which animal might be the perfect one to borrow.

Troy: Golly, there are so many interesting animals to choose from. I'll never be able to make a decision. . . . Hm, I know. I'll just ask who wants to be borrowed for a while.

Narrator: So Troy explains to the animals about the pet trick performance and how he has no pet and how he needs to just borrow one of them for a few days. And how much fun it will be . . . and all that. But the response was not one he was expecting. [TROY walks up to two ELEPHANTS.]

Elephant #1 [Talking from behind a "fence."]**:** Now son, let me get this straight. You want to borrow one of us so you can teach us a trick. A trick? Like, what kind of a trick?

Troy: Oh, I don't know, Maybe like sitting up on your hind legs and slowly turning your body around, like this. [TROY demonstrates.]

Elephants #1 and #2: You mean like this? [The ELEPHANTS sit up and turn their bodies around, and then laugh.]

Troy: Gosh, you already know how to do that?

[From another "cage," a HYENA speaks.]

Hyena: What other kinds of tricks do you have in mind, little boy?

Troy: Well, er, maybe I could tell a joke and my pet could laugh at it. Now that would be hard to do. That would be a real trick.

Hyenas #1 and #2: You mean like this? [All the HYENAS in the "cage" begin to laugh like hyenas.]

Troy [Dejectedly]**:** Laughing hyenas. I get your point.

Lion [From another "cage"]: You see son, what we are trying to say is that we, all of us, are considered the grandest, smartest, quickest of the animals. We are powerful, regal, brave, and strong. Doing a little old trick is, well . . .

Zebra [interrupting LION]: Frankly, it's silly. No, my boy, all we want to do is just watch people. Nothing more, nothing less. We want three square meals a day, a comfortable cage at night, and just being able to stand around and watch people.

[Song: WHO'S REALLY IN THE ZOO]

[At the conclusion of the song, the ZOO ANIMALS ad-lib wisecracks to the people who are watching them.]

Elephant #2: Hey, Charlie, look at the nose on that one.

Monkey: Listen to them chatter. Talk, talk, talk. That's all they do.

Troy [Loudly]: This is the worst idea I have ever had. (Exits.)

[As NARRATOR speaks, ZOO ANIMALS exit and PET STORE ANIMALS take their places on stage.]

Narrator: Well now, that was a disaster. But Troy didn't let it get to him too much. He immediately called up his second plan and headed straight for the place where he *knew* he could borrow a pet . . . the local pet store.

[Sound effect: Pet store sounds]

[PET STORE ANIMALS make loud animal sounds and begin a friendly attack on TROY, who ad-libs, "Down boy, atta girl, no, no," and so on.]

[Enter STORE OWNER.]

Store Owner [Holding bucket]: Feeding time. [ANIMALS make even louder sounds and follow the STORE OWNER off the stage.]

Troy: Never mind. Who am I kidding? [TROY walks to the front of the stage and sits, dejectedly.]

[Enter a SHAGGY DOG who comes on stage, looks around, and sniffs his way to TROY. He then lies down beside him and promptly closes his eyes.]

Troy: Hi, big ol' dog. Where did you come from? [Pats the dog's head.] You look as sad as I do. [DOG doesn't move or even open his eyes.] Boy, has this been a day. Have you ever wanted something really badly in your life and haven't been able to find it? Or even come close to finding it? It's not fun, I tell you. It's not fun. [TROY pats the dog's head again and just stares into space.]

Narrator: Troy and the dog sat side by side for a very long time, doing nothing but breathing. [BOTH breathe loudly.] And sighing. [BOTH sigh, TROY first, then the DOG.] Soon the sighs turned to yawns (BOTH yawn), then back to sighs (BOTH sigh), and finally back to breathing again (BOTH breathe]. After a while . . .

Troy [bolts upright]: I've got it! Why didn't I think of this before? [Turns to DOG.] YOU can be my pet. [Looks all over the DOG.] I don't see a collar, so you probably don't belong to anybody. [Opens the DOG'S mouth and winces.] Whew!!! I'll say you don't belong to anybody. When did you brush your teeth last? [DOG doesn't move.] This is great. This is the best. I can teach you hundreds of tricks, thousands of tricks, stupendous tricks, tricks that will change the universe. This will be the grandest moment of my life. Wait until I show all the kids in my class. . . . [Suddenly, the DOG sits up, scratches frantically, and saunters off.] Hey, come back. Come back here. Please come back. [DOG keeps walking offstage. TROY slumps back down, more dejected than ever.] I'll never have a pet. I'll never find anything to teach a trick to. [TROY begins to weep very silently, wiping tears gently away from his eyes.]

[From a backstage microphone, HARRIET'S voice appears.]

Harriet: I wouldn't be too sure about that.

Troy: [TROY looks up and around quickly, ready to fight.] Okay, you guys leave me alone. [TROY looks around and sees none of his classmates.] Now I am hearing things. [TROY begins to cry a bit more.]

Harriet [Coughs and clears her throat]**:** Excuse me. You *are* hearing things. [Coughs again.] You are hearing me.

Troy [Stops crying, looks around again]**:** Stephanie Lundsford, if that is you playing a trick on me, I swear I'll chase you around the school and . . .

Harriet: I don't believe that is necessary.

Troy [Still looking around]**:** I don't get it. *Who* are you? And *Where* are you? [TROY stands up and searches around the area.]

Harriet: Right down here. But be careful.

Troy: Where? Is that a magic trick or what? [Looks around and down on the floor.] All I see is a gum wrapper . . . a rock . . . and a . . . flea.

Harriet: That's me!

Troy [Picks up the gum wrapper]**:** A talking gum wrapper?

Harriet: No, no . . . over here.

Troy [picks up rock]**:** A talking rock?

Harriet [sighs heavily]**:** Boy, this is going to be harder than I thought. No, silly, over here . . . right next to your shoe.

Troy [bends down over his shoe and "picks up" the flea]**:** A flea? A [gulp] talking flea?

Harriet: Yep. That's me. Harriet Hazel Witherspoon IV. And you can move me just a bit more toward the middle of your hand, if you don't mind. A concussion hurts, you know.

Troy: I don't believe it. A talking flea?

Harriet: Happy to make your acquaintance. Er, uh . . . do you have a name?

Troy [in shock]**:** Oh, uh, Troy Alexander Humple III, to be exact. But you can call me Troy.

Harriet: And you can call me Harriet.

Troy: That's nice. . . . A talking flea?

Harriet: Among other things, my boy. I also can sing, dance, do gymnastics, play the piano, and I make a delicious peanut butter and banana sandwich with black olives.

Troy: But where did you come from?

Harriet: Quite simple, Troy. You said I could call you Troy, right? Well, I was just lounging around outside my house, which is located precisely on the neck of the dumb dog you were just sitting next to, when all of a sudden the dog started scratching. I lost my balance, went tumbling down to the pavement, and, well, the rest is history. So, in other words, you don't have to look anymore. Your problem is solved. Finis, done deal, it's a wrap, the end, search is over. You can now smile again . . . because, Troy Alexander Humple III, you finally have a . . . pet.

Troy: But it will never work. You are not a dog. You are not a cat or a parrot. You're not even a fish. You are a flea. Have you looked at yourself lately? You are a flea, Harriet. You are just a flea.

Harriet: And a smart one too, if you ask me. Now, if the two of us will just put our heads together [TROY tries], so to speak, we can think of a pet trick that will blow the entire school away. Are you willing?

Troy: Well, I don't know. It seems so impossible.

Harriet: There are many things that start out being impossible, Troy. And we will talk about that later. But right now, I'll ask my question again. Are you willing to be partners with me?

Troy [thinks and thinks]: Sure! I'll do anything. It's just that . . . gosh, this is about the craziest thing. . . Yes, Harriet, I'll do anything. I'll do whatever it takes. I want a pet more than I've ever wanted anything in my life. So . . . what do we do . . . partner?

Harriet: Well, Troy Alexander Humple III, this is going to take a little patience, a little luck, a little flea, a not so little boy, and a *whole lotta work*.

[Song: WHOLE LOTTA WORK]

[TROY exits at end of song.]

[UP MUSIC—set change to CLASSROOM.]

[Students are in the classroom working with their pets.]

Narrator: For the next few days, the boys and girls in Mrs. Thompson's third-grade class at _____ School didn't do too much math, or reading, or science, or art, or even PE. Instead, they spent most of their time rehearsing pet tricks with their pets. It was a very pleasant experience.

[UTTER CHAOS on stage.]

[Sound effects: Dogs barking, cats meowing, horses neighing, parrots screeching, snakes wrapped around MRS. THOMPSON'S body. Much confusion.]

Mrs. Thompson: All right, boys and girls, I think we are making progress here with these pets. Now if someone will gently unwrap Sam's pet snake from around my neck, we will begin rehearsing one more time starting with the first pet trick. Bring in the rooster.

[UTTER CHAOS reigns again as sound effects of different animals are played. TROY pantomimes his pet trick rehearsal in class with the rest of the class laughing silently.]

Narrator: The pet trick rehearsals continued, day after day, but every time Troy stood up to rehearse with Harriet, the rest of the class laughed so loudly that Troy had to stop what he was doing before he even finished his practice. [ALL exit except TROY.] Instead, he and Harriet waited 'till the classroom was empty before they practiced their special trick for the All-School Pet Trick Show.

Harriet: Okay, Troy, let's try it one more time. This time, you toss me up and I'll do three complete somersaults in the air before I land in your other hand. Okay? Here we go [Drum roll. TROY follows HARRIET'S "path" with his eyes.]

Troy: Harriet, that is amazing. How do you do that?

Harriet: It's all in the wrists, my boy, all in the wrists. Now, this time, you toss me up even higher and as I make five somersaults while in the air, I will sing "Way down upon the Swanee River." Okay?

[Sound effect: Drum roll]

Troy [in awe]: Whatever you say, Harriet. Are you ready? [Another drum roll. TROY "tosses" HARRIET up as HARRIET sings the song, then lands on TROY'S other outstretched palm.] That was magnificent, Harriet, more than magnificent, that was . . . impossible.

Harriet: Hard work. Remember? Now this time, Troy, you will toss me in the air, and I will do eight somersaults and then we will end with the pièce de résistance, a piano duet, you and me partner, playing "Chopsticks" for the entire world to hear. And since tomorrow is the All-School Pet Trick Show, we have got to get this part of the trick absolutely perfect.

Troy: Piano duet? Now you've really lost your mind, Harriet. You can't play the piano. Why, you are no bigger than a . . . flea.

Harriet: Troy Alexander Humple III, don't get sarcastic with me. If you remember, Napoleon wasn't the biggest person who ever lived. And what about Tom Thumb, or Michael J. Fox? Why, I can name hundreds of small . . .

Troy [interrupts HARRIET as he looks at his watch]**:** Oh, Harriet, it is almost 5:00. My mom will be furious if I'm late for dinner again. She hates reheating the soup, so I've got to run around the corner to the pay phone and call her to let her know I'm on my way. You stay right here, and I'll be back so we can rehearse our [cough] piano duet. Okay?

Harriet: That sounds good. But make it snappy! I've got some errands to run myself. Hurry up.

[TROY puts HARRIET down and runs off stage. A few seconds later, enter DOG, who saunters across the stage, scratches, and walks off.]

[Enter TROY.]

Troy: Okay, Harriet, I'm back. Come hop up in my hand so we can start practicing the duet. [Looks around.] Harriet? Hop up here so we can. . . . Harriet? Harriet? Where are you? [TROY becomes panicked.] Harriet, stop hiding. Where are you? We've got lots of work to do. [TROY begins to walk through the audience, calling out HARRIET'S name and looking for her in students' hair, pockets, collars, and so on.] *Harriet??? Where are you??? You can"t do this to me. Harriet??? Harriet???*

[UP MUSIC—as TROY exits through the audience looking for HARRIET.]

[Set change—All-School Pet Trick Show; microphone, piano/synthesizer, chairs on stage]

[CAST and MRS. THOMPSON enter, some as contestants, some as audience.]

Mrs. Thompson: All right, boys and girls, if we can find our seats, we'll begin. [CAST finds seats.] Good afternoon, everyone. At this time, I would like to introduce the wonderful principal of _____ School, Mr. Hogbottom.

[PRINCIPAL HOGBOTTOM comes to the podium/microphone.]

Principal Hogbottom: Ladies and gentlemen, boys and girls, I would like to welcome you to the first annual All-School Pet Trick Show here at _____ School. We are all very excited for the show to begin, so without further adieu, let us bring out our first contestant, Suzanne, and her parrot, Roscoe, who will give us his version of a Tarzan yell. [EVERYONE claps as SUZANNE, holding a fake bird on her shoulder, comes forward. Sound effect offstage of parrot preparing to yell like Tarzan. Midway though, the yell becomes a squawk, and then the parrot begins to screech. Both the parrot and Suzanne begin to scratch wildly.]

Principal Hogbottom: Well, Suzanne, unfortunately Roscoe wasn't quite able to finish. I am afraid we will have to go on to the next trick, and that would be Sam and his pet snake, Yolanda, who will shape its body into the word "Mississippi."

[Sound effect: Snake/flute music]

[SAM brings a long, stuffed snake in and begins shaping it, with helpers, into the letters M-I-S. Suddenly the snake begins to shake and is pulled off stage with SAM running after it, scratching wildly.]

Principal Hogbottom: How strange. Well, I am sure Sam will be able to catch Yolanda and come back on stage for the remainder of the program. Now on with the show. Next up will be Trish and her friends presenting her pet dog, Warren, doing a familiar cheer. ["Warren," a stuffed dog, is dressed in a cheerleader costume, as are the girls.]

Trish and Friends: Two bits, four bits, six bits, a dollar, all for the _____ [school mascot name], stand up and holler. ["Warren" howls, begins to scratch, and is yanked off the stage.]

Principal Hogbottom: Go get that dog!!! [Coughs.] Well, excuse me, now where was I? [A student, CARL, suddenly goes up to PRINCIPAL HOGBOTTOM and whispers in his ear.] Ladies and gentlemen, there has been a change in the program due to a bit of misfortune. Carl has just informed me that his pet rooster, George, will be unable to perform his trick of pretending to swim, because of a mysterious ailment that has just caused him to . . . scratch so hard that he . . . [gulps] has scratched all of his feathers off. [CARL holds up a rubber chicken.] I am so sorry, Carl. I guess that's show business. [CARL runs offstage.] So, ladies and gentlemen, that brings us, at last, to our final contestant in the All-School Pet Trick Show, Troy Humple, who will present his pet flea, Harriet . . . [ALL begin laughing and pointing at TROY.]

Troy: [TROY walks up to PRINCIPAL HOGBOTTOM.] I'm sorry, Mr. Hogbottom, but I don't have a pet . . . . You see, I had one, but it got lost and I've looked everywhere for it and . . .

Principal Hogbottom: What, my boy? No pet? Well, without a pet it seems as though you will be unable to continue in the All-School Pet Trick Show. And since none of the other contestants finished their portion, well, unfortunately, it is my sad duty to inform everyone that there will be no winner this year at the first ann . . . [Suddenly, "Chopsticks" (a tape of the song played offstage) begins playing. ALL gasp and look at the piano in amazement.]

TROY [grins and yells]: *Harriet!!!* [He runs to the piano, where he pantomimes playing the "Chopsticks" duet with her.]

[At the end of the song, ALL clap and yell, "Troy's the winner, Troy's the winner!" TROY "picks up" HARRIET and takes her back to PRINCIPAL HOGBOTTOM.]

Troy: Where did you go? I thought I'd lost you forever.

Harriet: Oh, sorry about that. When I saw the dog go by, I realized that I hadn't checked my e-mail messages in a while, so I hopped up into my house to do that and the dog took a wrong turn, and it took me a while to find you. . . . It's a long story, but it all turned out okay.

Principal Hogbottom: And the winner of the First Annual All-School Pet Trick Show is Troy Alexander Humple III and his pet flea, Harriet Hazel Witherspoon IV. [EVERYONE yells, claps, and picks up TROY.]

Mrs. Thompson [grabs the microphone]: And it also gives me great pleasure to share this bit of good news. Principal Hogbottom has just informed me that next year we will present _____ School's first Annual All-School Strangest Recipe Contest.

Troy [slowly looks up straight at the audience and smiles.]: Peanut butter and banana sandwich with olives. [And freezes.]

Narrator: You see, I told you he was like every other 8-year-old third-grade boy. . . . Well, almost.

THE END

[Finale: SMART PETS]

[Finale sung in audience.]

Pledge of Allegiance, Happy Birthday

spunky dunky

words/music by martha brady

Pledge of al le giance, hap py birth day, no one's tar dy, whose dog

is that, you look pret ty Mis ses Thomp son, get your math book out, let's

start. Sharp en pen cils, what's the wea ther, here's the lunch count, put the

ball up, no more talk ing, lost your glass es Miss es T?

Here's the hall pass, please spell Thurs day, don't lean back, hope lunch is

ta cos, some one's at the door please get it, that's my book, please give it

back. Sh' the in ter com, that's my ball, what page num ber, who is

ab sent, where's the ger bil, oh! you're new? Well, have a seat.

Ev ery day at school is a ka lei de

scope.   Such   a   big   sur   prise.

41

45

Ev ery min ute's diff erent and what's more, we

49

hope ad ven tures keep on com ing If they do, we'll

53

keep on hum ing Clap three times if you can hear me, spit your gum out,

57

put the glue up, turn to page one twen ty, close the binds, will you e

61

rase? What is smell ing, is that your ball, where's the chalk, it's time for

65

spe cials, not a fire drill, don't chew pa per Where's the place

69 piano solo

73

77

81
85
Ev ery day at school is a ka lei de
89
scope. Such a big sur prise.
93
Ev ery min ute's diff erent and what's more we
97
hope. ad ven tures keep on com ing, if they do we'll
101
keep on hum ming Face this way just turn your chair 'round. please don't hit, what
105
was the ques tion, here's a work sheet, I feel sick, the o ver head no
109
bulb. Trash can's full, have you got fe ver, who brought kit tens, don't have
113
pa per, sink is o ver flow ing, morn ing's just be gun.
117
Pledge of al legiance hap py birth day, morn ing's come.
121
Mis ses Thomp son you look love ly, school's
be gun.

Smart Pets

8-Beat Rock'n'Roll   words/music by martha brady

We got pets ___ that can sit up and beg ___ We got pets that can ___ scram ble an egg We got pets ___ that can yo - del and sing ___ We got pets ___ that can do an y thing We got pets

We got   Smart   Pets.

We got dogs that can read from a book.
We got birds than can learn how to cook.
We got snakes that can spell any word.
We got ducks that can act like a nerd.
We got pets. We got smart pets.

We got geese that can cough and can sneeze.
We got ants that can say, "thank you, please."
We got mice that can crochet and sew.
We got goats than can bowl like a pro.
We got pets. We got smart pets.

We got cows that can moonwalk a mile.
We got cats that can rhumba in style.
We got bats than can answer a phone.
We got worms that can act like Stallone.
We got pets. We got smart pets.

We got fish that can back up a car.
We got mules that can shoot golf at par.
We got squirrels that can make a souffle.
We got deer that play poker all day.
We got pets. We got smart pets.
We got pets. We got smart pets.
We got pets. We got smart pets.

When You Have A Dream

Brisk, if you get my drift   words/music by martha brady

When you have a dream and you know it's real. And you think it might come true. And your heart beats fast, and some how you feel that some bo dy needs to lis ten to your dream

When the ques tions come that you want to ask, and you know they might come true. And your eyes are wide, and you hope at last, that some bod y wants to lis ten to   your   dream.

But you   look   a   round   and you

see   no   one   an   y   where   And a

sad   ness   sur   rounds   you   and   co   vers   you   up from the

top   of   your   head   to   your   toes.   And you

want   just   one   friend,   who'll be

lieve   in   and   trust   you.   And you

wish   and   you   sigh.   And you

hope   and   you   cry.   And you

think   you   might   die,   for that

69
one dream. When you
73
have a dream, and it's yours a lone, and your
77
heart won't let it go. And you
81
want to smile, and you want to shout, and you
85
want some one to lis ten to your
89
dream But if
93
no one's there who will take the time. Who will
97
stop and say "I hear." Then your
101
dream will stay hid den deep in side, and there'll
105
be no room for an y more new

dreams.   And   there'll   be   no   room   for

an   y   more   new   dreams.

Who's Really In The Zoo

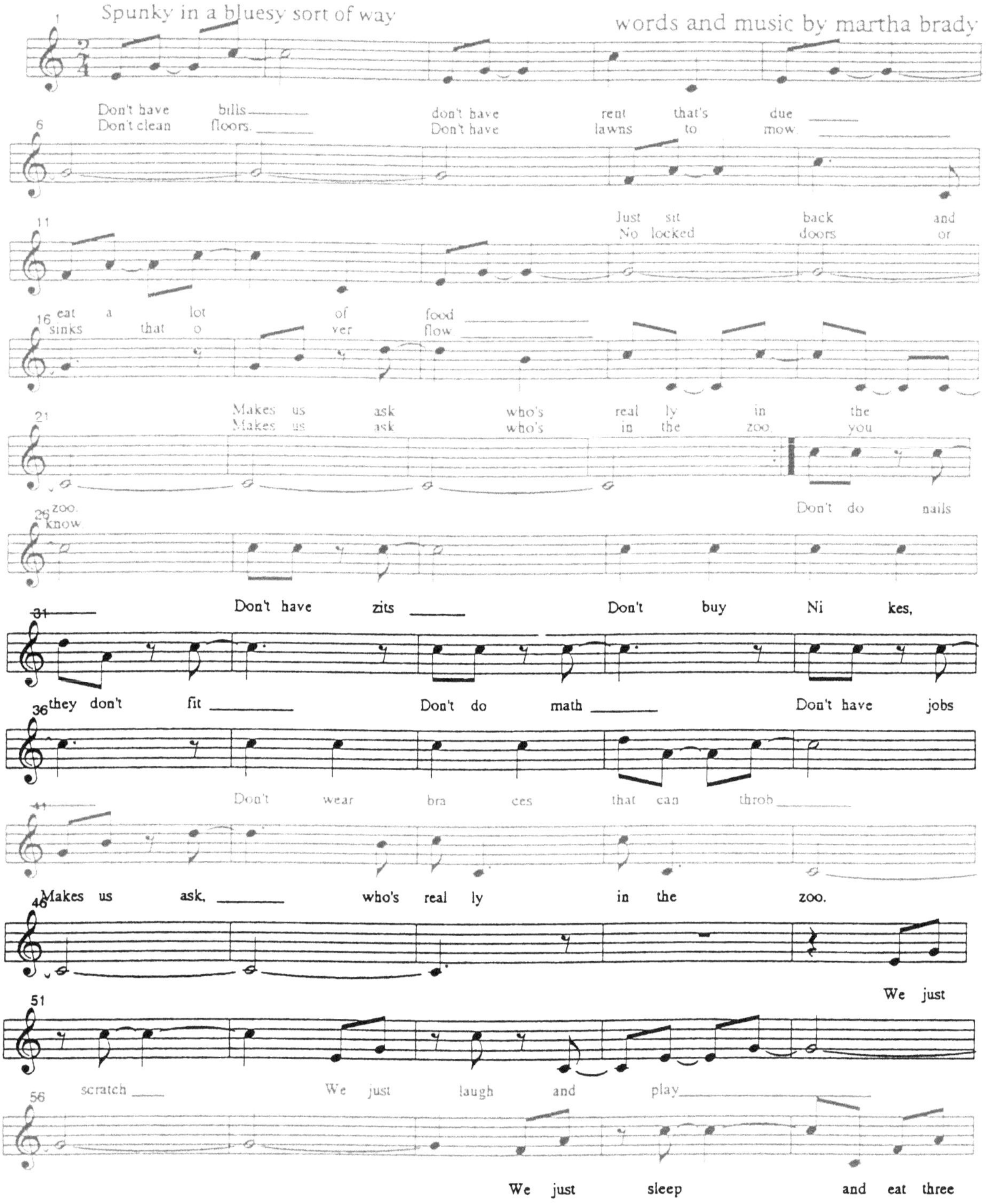

meals   a   We   all

know   who's   real   ly   in   the   zoo

Yes   we ____ know ____   whose   real   ly   in

the   zoo

Take   a ____ guess ____   We   think   it   might   be   you. ___

Whole Lotta Work

We're try ing some thing diff e rent that's nev er ever been

done. It may seem quite im poss i ble, no doubt, no

doubt. But with some grease and with some spit, we'll do our best to

con quer It. The two of us will make it all work out.

Verse 2 (Harriet)
It starts out by just being friends,
To that we've made a pact
It may be quite impossible to see, to see
But with a shake and with a grin,
We'll roll our sleeves and dig right in
There's one thing that the two of us agree

Verse 3 (Troy)
We've got a job before us
And it is gonna be hard
But we will put our noses to the stone, the stone
We'll grunt and sweat, we'll break our back
We'll never stop and that's a fact
One thing we know, it can't be done alone

Verse 4
(Troy) I'm counting on you, partner
(Harriet) You know that I'll be there
And we will do our best until we're through, we're through
With ups and downs, through thick or thin
In rain or snow, we'll fight to win
I'll always know that I can count on you

Next: During the course of rehearsals, students will continue to think about ways they persevere, take on tasks, and are responsible and accountable.

Then: Students will discuss personal experiences that occurred during the actual performance that required them to "step up and step out," which means meeting the challenge and doing the job required.

Finally: Students will write a reflective piece focusing on one thing they learned during the play experience that they did not know about themselves.

Alternative Assessment: None

✔ *And now, what about five good lessons from one good book?* See if these work.

The book: McCaughrean, Geraldine. Illustrated by Stephen Lambert. (2002). *My Grandfather's Clock*. New York: Clarion Books.

a. Place a plastic jar on a table. Tape a label on the jar that says, "What Can You Do in a Second?" All day Monday, students will write down on slips of paper things that can be done in only a second's time. At the end of the day, the teacher will read aloud some of the comments and students will discuss the feasibility of doing those things in the allotted time.

   As the week progresses, the label on the jar will be changed each day to include one of the following: "What Can You Do in a (minute, hour, day, week, month, or year)?"

b. Students will go on a playground field trip and watch the same shadows at certain times of the day. They will make inferences about what the shadows tell them about the time of day. Students may then create a poem that reinforces the information learned from those shadows.

c. Student will create personal charts or tables of how, without looking at a calendar, they know each day of the week. Below is a sample chart to help them along.

d. Create an interactive bulletin board. Students will bring found objects to place on the bulletin board that help them tell what season is in full swing at a particular time during the year.

e. Research clocks, such as Big Ben, that are found around the world. Brainstorm comparisons or factual statements to be placed on a chart. Some comparison or factual statements may include:

   1. Compare the sizes of the big clocks.

   2. Compare the towers in which the clocks usually sit.

Days of the Weeks	Telling Time without a Clock
Monday	Soccer practice
Tuesday	Piano lessons
Wednesday	Get a ride home from school with Aunt Jane
Thursday	Fast-food dinner because Mother works late
Friday	Scouts
Saturday	No school
Sunday	Grandparents come for dinner

3. Research the similarities in the mechanisms of the clocks.

4. Compare the ages of the big clocks.

5. Research events and circumstances that occurred to bring about the construction of the big clocks.

✔ *Oh yes. Remember the teachable moment* that introduced our activities in this chapter? Well, here is a little lesson to go with that idea.

Activity 5

Content: Science, Math

Lesson: Making Inferences, Predictions, and Assumptions

Standard: Students will understand that science involves asking and answering questions and comparing results to what is known.

Multiple Intelligences: Verbal/Linguistic: Students will ask and answer questions in a classroom discussion. Bodily/Kinesthetic: Students will construct machines from wood blocks. Interpersonal: Students will teach the class the function of one machine.

Materials: Simple and complex machines (e.g., stapler, pencil sharpener, window blinds, door knob, computer, television, video camera), wood blocks

Grade Level: 2–3

Objective: Students will brainstorm ways machines work. Students will create these machines from wood blocks.

Before: Students will show their expertise on one type of machine and teach the class how that particular machine works.

First: Students will look at machines found in and around the room. Students will make predictions, assumptions, and inferences about how these machines work.

Next: Students will be taught a lesson on how a stapler, clock, and/or pencil sharpener work. Students will create sequential charts of how these machines work.

Then: Students will choose one machine easily accessed in the room and, using the sequential charts, will recreate that machine from wood blocks.

Finally: Students will reflect upon one machine used widely at home and its impact on the daily lives of their family.

Alternative Assessment: Students will choose one machine found in the room and research that machine in regard to changes in design and function occurring with that machine over time.

✔ And finally, if you think *a picture is worth a thousand words,* use the *Machines* drawing on the next page to engage your students in seeing, writing, drawing, or just thinking about machines, technology, and the ways our lives are made easier by them. The activities connected to this drawing should work wonders for boys and girls who love to know how things work and who enjoy those workings even better if they can see them through color, shape, form, and design.

Activity 6

Content: Technology

Lesson: How Things Work

Standard: Students will communicate about internal technology operations using developmentally appropriate and accurate terminology.

Multiple Intelligences: Verbal/Linguistic: Students will use speaking and communication skills. Logical/Mathematical: Students will formulate opinions.

Materials: Copies of machines drawing

Grade Level: 1–3

Objective: Students will formulate opinions of how things work and share those opinions verbally with the class.

Before: Give students a chance to look at several children's books relating to "how things work." Choose one machine from one of the books, and lead a discussion on its function and method of working.

First: Students will choose one machine from the machines drawing. They will jot down notes about how they think the machine functions before they share that information with the rest of the class.

Next: Using their notes, students will explain how, in their opinion, their machine works.

Then: Lead a Q & A session about each machine. Limit the students to two questions they can ask each other about particular machines.

Finally: Choose a machine from the drawing and reflect upon it with this question: "The _____ (machine) is important in my life because _____."

Alternative Assessment: Assign a short research paragraph about the machines chosen from the drawings.

Activity 7

Content: Arts

Lesson: Pantomiming Machines

Standard: Students will create scenarios in which inanimate objects connect with animate objects.

Multiple Intelligence: Bodily/Kinesthetic: Students will pantomime action.

Materials: None

Grade Level: 3

Objective: Students will use their bodies to become inanimate objects.

Before: Pick one inanimate object from the classroom (chair). Students will use their bodies to "become the chair" and give it human action.

First: Students will pair up and select one machine from the machines drawing. One student will become the machine. The other will remain human. Both students will interact with each other as "machine and human." For example, one student may use his body to become a lawn mower. The other student will use the human lawn mower to "mow" the room.

Next: Lead a discussion on impressions students had when they acted like machines as opposed to when they acted like humans.

Then: Students will think of machines not found in the machines drawing. They will use art paper to draw the machines. Other paired students will act out those machines.

Finally: Students will reflect upon a machine at home that seems to do human tasks.

Alternative Assessment: In groups, students will create a scenario with a beginning, middle, and end in which several machines are part of the scenario. Other students guess the mystery machines depicted in the scenarios.

Activity 8

Content: Language Arts

Lesson: Onomatopoeia

Standard: Students will create onomatopoeias.

Multiple Intelligences: Visual/Spatial: Students will use visual art as a stimulus for writing. Verbal/Linguistic: Students will use appropriate spelling and writing skills.

Materials: Copies of machines drawing

Grade Level: 2–3

Objective: Students will create onomatopoeic words to accompany machines found in the machines drawing.

Before: Find three machines in the room. Let the students hear the sounds they make. Students will recreate these sounds with their own voices and try to spell those sounds.

First: Students will use the use the following matching sheet to practice matching the machines found on the machines drawing with the sounds they make. Once the matching sheet has been completed, students will create their own worksheet of matching machines to sounds.

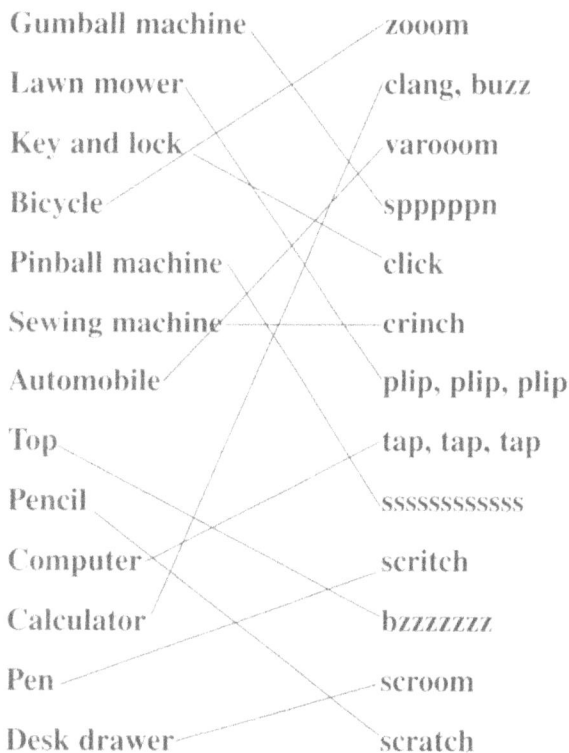

Gumball machine	zooom
Lawn mower	clang, buzz
Key and lock	varooom
Bicycle	sppppn
Pinball machine	click
Sewing machine	crinch
Automobile	plip, plip, plip
Top	tap, tap, tap
Pencil	sssssssssss
Computer	scritch
Calculator	bzzzzzzz
Pen	scroom
Desk drawer	scratch

Next: Students will make a list of the machines and create their own "matching machine to sound" worksheet.

Then: The sheets will be collected and redistributed to the students who will work on someone else's worksheet. Worksheets will be shared and discussed.

Finally: Students will reflect upon sounds that come from machines with which they are familiar.

Alternative Assessment: Students will write paragraphs omitting words and replacing omitted words with onomatopoeic words.

Activity 9

Content: Language Arts, Arts

Lesson: Telling Stories

Standard: Students will prepare and deliver information to an audience.

Multiple Intelligences: Verbal/Linguistic: Students will tell a story. Visual/Spatial: Students will use a design to assist in implementing a story.

Materials: Copies of machines drawing, art paper, crayons

Grade Level: 2–3

Objective: Students will draw any kind of picture and add one of the machines in the machines drawing to the picture. Students will write or tell a story using the information from these pictures.

Before: Students will draw pictures of any kind and add one machine from the machines drawing to these pictures.

First: The pictures will be redistributed to the class. Students will title the picture they are given. The pictures will be redistributed again. Students will write or tell a story using someone else's picture and title as a catalyst.

Next: The original owners of the pictures will briefly tell the stories they had in mind when drawing the pictures.

Then: Comparisons will be made between the original story concept and the stories told by other students.

Finally: Students will write their own stories to their own pictures.

Alternative Assessment: None

Activity 10

Content: Math

Lesson: Categorizing

Standard: Students will use manipulatives to count, order, and group.

Multiple Intelligence: Logical/Mathematical: Students will put in order and categorize.

Materials: Copies of machines drawing

Grade Level: K

Objective: Students will use the machines in the machines drawing to put objects in order, to group, and to count.

Before: Students will look at the machines drawing and count and name each machine on the drawing.

First: Students will cut out each machine, place the pieces on their desks, and put them in order according to:

   a. alphabetical order
   b. size
   c. weight
   d. difficulty to operate
   e. other

Next: Students will discuss different ways to sort, group, and categorize these machines.

Then: Students will spend time on their own to categorize or sort the machine pictures any way they wish.

Finally: Students will look at each machine and complete this sentence: "A _____(machine) looks like a _____."

Alternative Assessment: Students will pick one machine and think of different machines that are similar in function to that one machine.

Activity 11

Content: Language Arts

Lesson: Telling Stories

Standard: Students will use effective vocabulary and organization to relate information.

Multiple Intelligences: Visual/Spatial: Students will use the machines drawing as a stimulus for telling a story. Verbal/Linguistic: Students will tell a story. Intrapersonal: Students will reflect upon past experiences.

Materials: Copies of the machines drawing

Grade Level: K–3

Objective: Students will look at the different elements of the drawing in this chapter and tell an original story.

Before: Students will review important aspects of telling a story.

First: Students will use the machines drawing as a stimulus for telling stories about different experiences happening in the scenes in the picture.

Next: Students will relate personal stories that correspond to the original stories being told.

Then: Students will answer "What would happen if . . . " questions about the picture.

Finally: Students will reflect upon their own appreciation of the drawing.

Alternative Assessment: Students will take a drawing home and ask a family member to tell them a story that comes from viewing the drawing.

To wrap up this chapter, here is every idea you ever wanted to know about machines. Maybe now is the time to tinker with some ideas about how things work.

Machines K–3

V/L	Find five simple machines in the classroom. Give opinions of how they work.	Keep a list of all the machines you use in a day. Make a master list in class.	"Talk" machines.	Write about its function.	Read *The Little Engine that Could* and other books about working machines.
L/M	Dismantle a pencil sharpener or clock. Give logical reasons for their functions.	Beginning at the top of your head, say all the moving parts in your own "human machine."	With a fifth- or sixth-grade buddy, brainstorm "future machines."	Compare manual and electric pencil sharpeners.	Think of a riddle that describes a machine in the classroom.
V/S	Draw a machine that can be used in the classroom. Label its parts.	Use several pictures of machine parts to montage one original machine.	Watch the movie *Chitty Chitty Bang Bang*.	Draw yourself.	Collect pictures of difference machines to use in Machine Pictionary.
B/K	Use your friends to act out the machine.	In groups of three, create one original machine that makes life easier.	Demonstrate how the moving parts work.	Construct a machine of the future.	Act out household appliances.
M/R	Listen to a tape of machine sounds.	Use the song, "The Wheels on the Bus," to write a song about machine parts.	Compose a melody using machine sounds.	Learn work-related songs. Example, "I've Been Working on the Railroad."	Create original sounds that fit the machine.
Inter	In teams, play Machine Pictionary.	Select one machine. Teach the class how it works.	Teach the class a song about work.	Teach the class its function.	Help a buddy make a machine out of Legos, wood blocks, or cardboard boxes.
Intra	Keep a machine log of the machines you use on a daily basis.	Journal about your reactions to the different sounds.	"What machine are you most like, and why?"	Think about one machine that is now obsolete. Why is that so? What took its place?	"If you could be a machine for one day, what would it be, and why?"
N	Take a field trip outside. Look for and discuss nature's machines.	Explain how an ant might be a machine.	Investigate how cars affect the environment.	Relate machines to farms, dairies, apple orchards, and other grade-specific topics.	Create a food machine that grows food in an unconventional way.

The activities and experiences in this grid are just a bit more difficult and can bring some challenges to your students. These ideas can be used as extension lessons or individual projects, or, in some cases, in learning centers.

Machines 4–6

V/L	Write a story about how you would live in the twenty-first century with no machines.	Read and discuss *Machines*, by Fred Wilkin, and *The Amazing Pop-Up Book*, by Jay Young.	Select one machine found in the classroom. Debate its importance.	Pick three specific questions to ask a mechanic about a car.	Write a "How to" manual for this machine.
L/M	Create a timeline of machines from a historical perspective.	Create an assembly line system to create a new product.	Compare significant technologies among countries.	Use computational skills to keep track of changes in certain machine designs.	Design and construct a machine for an invention convention.
V/S	Create an art transformation with a machine focus.	Mind-map the word machine.	Design a brochure.	Construct a diorama whose focus is tools from ancient times.	Interpret Rube Goldberg machine drawings.
B/K	Play Machine Jeopardy.	Research the Internet for machines that have affected history in significant ways.	Pantomime historical moments that relate to machines.	From found objects, construct a machine that can stop pollution.	On a walking field trip around the school, make conclusions about machines observed.
M/R	Create a sequencing rap about the function of a clock.	Show how certain sounds come from certain musical instruments.	Use machine sounds to decipher patterns.	Create a sound onomatopoeia rap.	Write an original song about a simple machine.
Inter	Lead a discussion about the perfect machine.	Create a junk machine that solves a problem found in the book, *Cloudy with a Chance of Meatballs*.	Research the shark as the ultimate eating machine.	Assist in the design and implementation of an invention convention.	Brainstorm an ad campaign to sell a "new" household appliance.
Intra	Reflect upon certain machines and their impact on your life.	"The one machine that does the most harm/good in my life is the _____ because _____."	What inventor should be called the Father of Inventions? Why?	What machine would you like to invent? Why?	Why does a car need gas to function?
N	Compare the life cycles of a human and of one of nature's machines.	Equate the Machine Age with the decline of the environment.	Explain the significance of five medical machines and their connection to our survival.	Study the evolution of one machine.	Global technology: explain how it affects you and your family.

PATTERNS

Dear Teacher,

Patterns are everywhere. They are our breath, our walk, and our way of eating dinner. They are clouds above our heads, gravel beneath our feet, and freckles on our arms. Patterns are numbers and music. They are heartbeats and the act of running. Patterns are parking spaces and traffic jams. They are cans on grocery shelves. They are green beans in the cans.

Patterns are rivers and deserts, birds' nests and prairie dog holes. Patterns are snowflakes and snow tracks, raindrops and umbrellas. They are sound waves and ocean waves, stairs going up and stairs going down. They are visual and olfactory, auditory and tactile. And there are as many ways to bring patterns to children's lives as there are patterns themselves.

So let us begin our first lesson on patterns with the pattern of the poem in this introductory letter. Write the poem on chart paper and leave out some important words. Ask students to find the sound patterns that will fit in the place of the missing words.

Inside Patterns

Books on shelves, carpet on floors
Frames on windows, hinges on doors.
Notebook pages, slats on blinds
Numbers on clocks, counting time.
Stars on flags, coats on racks,
Jellybean jars, chairs that stack.
Words on blackboards, kids in rows
Glue in cupboards, socks on toes.
Illustrations, pencils in cups
Tiles on ceilings, just look up
Legs on tables, arms on desks
Won't these patterns take a rest?
Stripes on blouses, shoes on feet
Golden freckles start to repeat
Patterns here, patterns there
Look around and show me where

After the students have read the poem, lead them on a scavenger hunt around the room looking for all the patterns the poem describes. Then create an activity with each of the patterns that they see. For example, here are some suggestions for the following classroom patterns as stated in the poem:

1. Books on shelves: Use one shelf of books. Create patterns according to color, size, and so on.

2. Carpet on floors: Find the patterns in the carpet in your classroom. Compare with patterns found in a book of carpet squares you can borrow from a carpet store.

3. Frames on windows: Draw the patterns that are created by the window frames in your classroom. Continue the scavenger hunt around the room and find other objects that have similar square or rectangle patterns to the window frames.

4. Hinges on doors: Make comparisons of all the hinges found in the classroom. What do these hinge patterns have in common? How are they different? Where might you find hinges in the classroom? Where might you find hinges outside the classroom?

5. Notebook pages: Ask students to find different patterns of paper in their own notebooks or in chapters from their textbooks. They may look for chapter headings, chapter format, and chapter endings. Ask students to describe the repetitions they observe in those notebook or textbook pages.

6. Slats on blinds: Find examples of clothing children are wearing that are similar to the patterns found when the classroom blinds are open, then closed. Create shadow patterns with the blinds.

7. Numbers on clocks: Ask students to draw a clock or watch they have in their homes. The drawings will then be compared according to patterns seen in the various clocks or watches around the classroom.

8. Stars on flags: Look at the pattern of stars on the American flag. Compare that pattern with patterns found in state or other country flags.

9. Coats on racks: Once a week, a group of students will be responsible for creating a pattern of some kind with the coats hanging on the racks. These patterns could be color based, length based, or even alphabetical, according to owner.

10. Jellybean jars: Observe and discuss hidden patterns found in a jar of jellybeans.

11. Chairs that stack: One pod of students will stack their pod chairs into some pattern. Other pods will try to duplicate the pattern they see.

12. Words on blackboards: Write a selection of words on the blackboard that have observable patterns (e.g., words with double consonants; words that end in silent *e* or *ing*; words that have one vowel, two vowels, or three vowels; nonsense words that have patterns; and so on). Students will figure out the patterns.

13. Kids in rows: Students will line up in rows of six or eight. They will create body patterns while standing in a row. Other children will figure out the patterns.

14. Glue in cupboards: Students will simply look in cupboards to see if there is a pattern in how the teacher stores supplies, including glue.

15. Socks on toes: Students will use their stocking feet to create various patterns.

16. Illustrations: Students will look through various children's picture books and discuss and compare various patterns found in the illustrations of these picture books.

17. Pencils in cups: If children keep pencils, markers, pens, and so on in cups on each pod table, ask students to rearrange those items into a plausible pattern. Other students will duplicate the various patterns.

18. Tiles on ceilings: Students will find patterns in one ceiling tile, in rows of ceiling tiles, and in the entire ceiling of tiles.

19. Legs on tables: Write a point of view story about being a leg on a table and why there is a pattern of four legs on a table, rather than two or three or six.

20. Arms on chairs: Observe the classroom as a whole. Note the arms on the desks. Students will write about what they think the arms represent.

21. Stripes on blouses: Make comparisons of patterns found on blouses or T-shirts the children are wearing. Create a clap pattern that defines the different patterns.

22. Shoes on feet: Sorry. I had to have a word that came close to rhyming with "repeat."

23. Freckles: Students will look at their own hands, legs, arms, or faces to find patterns in freckles.

Well, now, this looks like a good beginning to your unit or lessons on patterns. And if these twenty-three ideas are not enough to get you started, we haven't even gone outside yet.

Teachable moments often come when your hands are full of manipulatives for a math lesson on base 10. You trip over a book on the floor and out of your grasp flies a bag of buttons you bought at Wal-Mart and a box of round toothpicks you found behind the salt and pepper shakers in your kitchen cabinet. The button bag splits open on impact, the toothpick box lid flips open as it hits the carpet. And in an instant, you have the makings of a brilliant lesson on patterns. A teachable moment has fallen into your life, and you are ever so pleased.

Activity 1

Content: Math

Lesson: Charting Patterns in Food

Standards: Students will create, describe, and extend a variety of patterns, using concrete objects. Students will sort and classify objects and patterns according to observable attributes.

Multiple Intelligences: Visual/Spatial: Students will recognize certain objects and discern similarities among them. Logical/Mathematical: Students will organize a set of objects into some reasonable form.

Materials: Food items

Grade Level: 1–3

Objective: The students will use various food items to observe patterns formed and/or placed in these items. Students will create charts from this information.

Before: Bring an orange to class. Cut it into halves. Ask the children to tell everything they *know to be true* as they observe the inside of the orange and the outside as well.

First: Bring a pomegranate and a bunch of red grapes to class. Students will discuss the similarities in the structure and pattern of both fruits. Students will make a list of other fruits that grow in bunches. Teacher will show bunches of bananas, carrots, radishes, and so on for children to observe and compare.

Next: Show the patterns found on the inside of apples, squash, bananas, starfruit, kiwi, and so on. Also show the patterns found on the outside of pineapple, celery, artichoke, onion, cactus leaf, asparagus, and corn on the cob. Students will discuss, describe, and compare these patterned fruits.

Then: Students will categorize these foods into similar patterns.

Finally: Students will take a trip to the grocery store, either with the family or as a class field trip, where they will observe patterns found in canned goods (pickles, asparagus, okra spears), cookies (round, stacked, squares, sprinkled), soda cans, and pasta (spaghetti, penne, gemelli, egg noodles, and so on). The students will then compare patterns found in the grocery store to patterns found in the classroom or in the school building.

Alternative Assessment: Students will use wood blocks, pipe cleaners, buttons, stones, geometric-shaped cardboard cutouts, and other manipulatives to re-create patterns found in specified fruits and vegetables that come to mind from the following rhyming clues:

    a. Cut an apple. Don't look far. Right inside you'll find a _____. (Star)

    b. Round and black, white in the middle. Chocolate tasting is this riddle. (Oreo cookie)

    c. _____, _____. Yum. Yum. Are you ready? (Spaghetti)

    d. Stones that are worn. A cob full of _____. (Corn)

Activity 2

Content: Math

Lesson: Patterns and Rhythm/Music

Standard: Create, describe, and extend a variety of patterns using shapes, events, designs, and numbers.

Multiple Intelligences: Musical/Rhythmic: Students may hear a certain rhythm or tune (melody) and group that rhythm or tune with similar rhythms or tunes. Bodily/Kinesthetic: Students may use their hands in a skillful way to create appropriate hand-jive patterns.

Materials: Classical music, sticks, empty cardboard boxes

Grade Level: 2–4

Objective: Students will listen to various selections of music to discern musical patterns and create patterned chants, hand-jives, and name ostinatos.

Before: Discuss the statement, "If something happens three or more times, it is considered a pattern." Look around the room to find something that occurs three or more times. Now ask the students what things they do each and every morning to get ready for school. Discuss how just doing something over and over can create patterns. Lastly, with the children, sing three verses to "Old McDonald Had a Farm." Discuss how each verse has the same melody. Relate this to patterns.

First: Play excerpts from three pieces of classical music (e.g., Bach, Beethoven, and Brahms). Discuss the different instrumental patterns in all three. See if the students can hear the different instruments. Then play three excerpts from three different vocal performers. Include a rap in one of the excerpts. See if the students can hear the diverse patterns in the words and vocal melody for each song.

Next: Students will use sticks, dowels, or pencils to create patterns with a call/response technique. Make a sound pattern hitting two pencils, dowels, or sticks together. Children will duplicate the pattern they hear. They will create their own patterns for other children to duplicate.

Then: In groups, students will use their first names to create a patterned ostinato (musical sequence). Using empty boxes for drums, students will clap a steady beat as they call out their different names in some patterned sequential order. Example: Mar-i-lyn, Mi-chael, Ro-bert, Jane / Mar-i-lyn, Mi-chael, Ro-bert, Jane / and so on.

Finally: Students will choose a nursery rhyme and clap the beat of the nursery rhyme, using this method to discern the pattern of the nursery rhyme.

Alternative Assessment: Students, in groups, will create an original patterned hand-jive with the following suggested topics: cars, fruit, weather, sports, trees, animals, vowels, songs, and so on. A sample hand-jive about fruit and the pattern formula looks like this:

A A E E
A A E E
A A E E
I I O O U
A A E E
A A E E
A A E E
I I O O U

Avocado, Avocado, Banana, Banana
Avocado, Avocado, Banana, Banana
Avocado, Avocado, Banana, Banana
Kiwi, Kiwi, Mango, Mango, Orange
Avocado, Avocado, Banana, Banana
Avocado, Avocado, Banana, Banana
Avocado, Avocado, Banana, Banana
Kiwi, Kiwi, Mango, Mango, Orange

Activity 3

Content: Math, Language Arts

Lesson: Patterns and Movement

Standards: Create, describe, and extend a variety of patterns using shapes, events, designs, and numbers. Use correct spelling punctuation, capitalization, grammar, and word usage to effectively complete a variety of writing tasks.

Multiple Intelligences: Bodily/Kinesthetic: The students will create dance movements that have purpose, intention, and rhythm. Verbal/Linguistic: Students will use a combination of words for a specific occasion.

Materials: Musical selections, list of action words

Grade Level: 1–4

Objective: Students will use their bodies to create appropriate definitions for various action words (locomotor movements).

Before: Read any of Dr. Seuss's books. They are filled with action words. Some are real, and others are nonsensical. Either or both kinds of words work well for this preliminary activity.

First: Children will brainstorm all the action words they know from reading a Dr. Seuss book. These words will be placed on the board.

Next: Students will listen to music and use their bodies to create the appropriate actions of these words. Be sure to place several nonsensical words on the board so that children must create their own meaning of the words before they can transfer that meaning to movement.

Then: Students will choose four action words and create an action pattern from these words. An example might be to spin three times, bounce one time, hop three times, bounce one time, skip three times, and bounce one time. This action "sentence" will be repeated over and over. Other students will try to duplicate various patterns.

Finally: Students will transfer the action sentences to a poetry exercise using various action words in the same pattern to which they moved their bodies. A sample poem using the above action words might be:

> The spinning leaves, the spinning leaves, the spinning leaves
> Bounce to the ground
> The hopping clouds, the hopping clouds, the hopping clouds
> Bounce around the sky
> The skipping children, the skipping children, the skipping children
> Bounce home for dinner.

Alternative Assessment: The students will write their poems and draw pictures to illustrate their poems. The poems and illustrations will be collected into a class poetry book entitled *Movement and Patterns.*

Activity 4

Content: Math, Language Arts

Lesson: Patterns in Creative Writing

Standards: Read and comprehend consumer information such as forms, newspaper ads, warning labels, and safety pamphlets. Use the writing process to complete effectively a variety of writing tasks. Recognize that patterns can emerge from a variety of real-world situations.

Multiple Intelligences: Verbal/Linguistic: Students will communicate, through writing, a set of ideas. Bodily/Kinesthetic: The students will demonstrate the capacity to manufacture an object with the use of tools.

Materials: Newspapers

Grade Level: 3+

Objective: Students will write patterned ads from a list of assigned topics.

Before: Generate a discussion on the power of advertisements. Ask leading questions regarding exact student purchases and purchases related to clothing, cereal, and so on.

First: Students will look through newspaper ads and cut out several that appeal to them as interesting, unique, lyrical, and so on. Students will discuss any word patterns that occur in these advertisements.

Next: Students, in groups, will select a topic from the list written on the board and create a patterned ad or jingle that sells that particular object. Suggested topics include socks, a golden retriever puppy, a candy bar, a box of cereal, the number 10, and bottled water.

Then: The students will construct the particular object or item about which the ad was written.

Finally: The students will create a display area for the ad campaign.

Alternative Assessment: Students will "sell" their items.

Activity 5

Content: Math, Science, Language Arts

Lesson: Creative Writing with Patterns and Art and Architecture

Standard: Formulate generalizations about patterns. Create, describe, and extend a variety of patterns using shapes and so on. Write a creative story that has a beginning, middle, and end.

Multiple Intelligence: Visual/Spatial: The students will be able to perceive the visual world accurately and re-create aspects of that visual experience.

Materials: Pictures of early structures, art work

Grade Level: 3–4

Objective: Students will find and discuss patterns in art. Students will locate architectural patterns found in and around the school building. Students will write a story about "a perfect structure."

Before: Students will be shown various pictures of well-known architectural structures including the White House, Roman Coliseum, Stonehenge, Golden Gate Bridge, and other age-appropriate structures. Students will discuss the repetitive patterns found in each structure.

First: Students will go on an architectural field trip around the school, seeking evidence of repetitive patterning in the architecture of the building.

Next: Students will compare and contrast the architectural patterns found in the early well-known structures and those found in the school building.

Then: Students will look at pictures of different well-known works of art and make comparisons of patterns found in all three areas: art, school architecture, and early structures.

Finally: Using information gathered about architectural patterns, students will write a story or paragraph about living in a perfect structure.

Alternative Assessment: After completing the written assignment, students will use that writing piece as a guide for drawing or constructing that perfect structure.

Activity 6

Content: Science, Language

Lesson: Creative Writing with Patterns in Nature

Standards: Ask questions about the natural world. Use correct spelling, punctuation, capitalization, grammar, and word usage to complete a writing task.

Multiple Intelligences: Visual/Spatial: Students will be able to produce a graphic likeness from spatial information. Verbal/Linguistic: Students will construct phrases.

Materials: Pattern booklets, pictures of nature's patterns, digital cameras

Grade Level: 3+

Objective: Students will familiarize themselves with the various patterns found in nature and will create reflective pieces about specific patterns.

Before: Students will look at the photographs of nature's patterns in the following book and develop a basic understanding of the different types of patterns found in nature.

Murphy, P., and W. Neil. (1993). *By Nature's Design.* San Francisco: Chronicle Books.

First: Students will have a booklet of pages with one of the following natural design headings on each of the pages: spirals, meanders, curves, florets, radiations, helixes, cells, fractals, rosettes, channels, ripples, chambers, branchings, orbs, crags, and whorls.

Next: Students will take the booklets outside and try to find as many of nature's patterns as possible. They will take some science field notes for each pattern observed, and draw a likeness of that specific pattern.

Then: As the week or month progresses, students will select one pattern per day or week and write short, reflective pieces about the patterns. These written pieces can be cinquains, quotes, simple phrases, or free verse.

Finally: Students will again go outside with their booklets. Each student will choose one of nature's patterns to observe, and read the appropriate reflective piece to the rest of the class.

Alternative Assessment: Students will use a camera to create a montage of one particular pattern from nature. These montages will be used as a background for an interactive bulletin board.

✔ *And now, what about five good lessons from one good book?* See if these work.

The book: Prelutsky, Jack. Illustrations by Petra Mathers. (2002). *The Frog Wore Red Trousers*. New York: Greenwillow Books.

1. Read *The Frog Wore Red Trousers*. Look for patterned cadence in the poetry. Find poems that have the same cadence. Clap the cadences as you read the poems. Make a list of all the national monuments found in Prelutsky's book. Use the Internet to research a monument not found in the book. Using a patterned cadence you like, write a short poem about that monument. Again, collect the poems to create a class booklet.

2. Take the structure from the poem *The Frog Wore Red Trousers*. Rewrite it to fit your own interest. Here is an example. (Remember, I have cats.)

   There was a tiny kitty

   Who learned to say his vowels.

   He jumped around and played all day

   Without those kitty howls.

   he liked to sit upon my lap

   And curl up for a rest.

   Then out popped A, E, I, O, U.

   From where? I have no guess.

3. Find poems that have some alliteration in the titles, such as "Barnaby Boone" and "Sarah Small." Write nonsense alliteration phrases by having students choose one alliteration letter of the alphabet. Each student will write one action word that begins with that letter on a slip of paper. Those slips are placed in a container. Each student will write two nouns that begin with that letter on two slips of paper. Those slips are placed in another container. Each student will write three adjectives that begin with that letter on three slips of paper. Those slips are placed in yet another container. Students now create their own alliteration name that begins with the chosen letter of the alphabet, and then draw a verb, three adjectives, and two nouns. With those words, they create an original alliteration. To create a pattern, have the students write the alliteration phrase three times, then create an ending fourth line. An example might be:

   Barnaby Boone baked black, beautiful, bashful basketballs and bananas.

   Barnaby Boone baked black, beautiful, bashful basketballs and bananas.

   Barnaby Boone baked black, beautiful, bashful basketballs and bananas.

   Barnaby Boone, Barnaby Boone, Barnaby Boone, Barnaby Boone

4. In the book, there are many poems about actual places in the United States. There are poems about South Dakota, Seattle, Indianapolis, San Jose, Winnemucca, and Tucumcari, to name a few. With a partner, write a poem about your own town or city. Create a class mural of your town. Type the poems on a computer and arrange them around the mural.

5. To throw a bit of social studies into the scheme of things, look in Jack Prelutsky's book one more time for actual towns and cities in the United States. Find these on the U.S. map. Research one interesting fact about each town or city. This has little to do with patterns, but it should be interesting for the students to attempt.

✓ *Oh yes. Remember the teachable moment* that introduced our activities in this chapter? Well here is a little lesson to go with that idea.

Activity 7

Content: Math, Language Arts

Lesson: Following Directions

Standard: Students will formulate generalizations of patterns.

Multiple Intelligences: Logical/Mathematical: Students must use reasoning abilities. Visual/Spatial: Students must think in terms of images.

Materials: Toothpicks, buttons

Grade Level: 2–4

Objective: The students will listen to directions and use toothpicks and buttons to create patterns.

Before: Ask half the class to pick up the buttons that have been scattered all over the room and to put them in a container. The other half of the class will pick up the toothpicks that are lying in all four corners of the room. They will place them in a container as well.

First: Give a brief review of the definitions of "horizontal" and "vertical." Then, as all the children look on, give simple directions on how to create a square using toothpicks. Be sure to incorporate horizontal and vertical directions. After the square is modeled, students will create a square out of toothpicks. Now, give simple directions on how to create a triangle with toothpicks, and also add three buttons on each corner of the square. Children will do likewise.

Next: Students will spend time creating their own free patterns with toothpicks and buttons.

Then: Give sequential directions. Students will create patterned designs that come from those directions. Sample sequential directions may be:

1. Line up, horizontally, one row of buttons with five buttons in that row.

● ● ● ● ●

2. Line up two more rows of button horizontally, with five buttons in each of those rows.

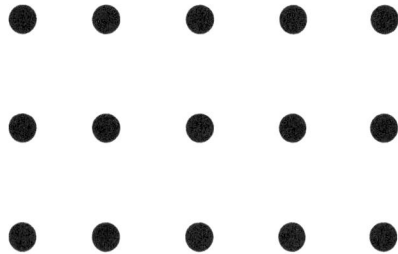

● ● ● ● ●

● ● ● ● ●

● ● ● ● ●

3. Underneath the middle button on the bottom row, line up three buttons in one vertical row.

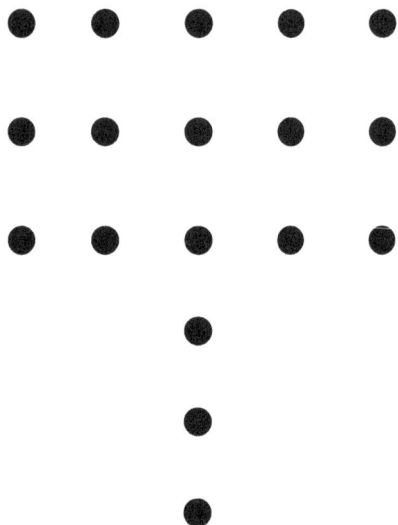

● ● ● ● ●

● ● ● ● ●

● ● ● ● ●

　　　●

　　　●

　　　●

Finally: Students will pair up as one student gives directions and one student creates the pattern from those directions.

Alternative Assessment: This isn't an assessment as much as it is simple fun. Read a children's book. Any book will do. As you read, stop along the way and ask students to use toothpicks and/or buttons to create a scene or object you describe from the book. Or better yet, as you read, stop along the way and ask students to use the toothpicks and buttons to create something that will solve a problem presented in the book or will help the story along.

✔ And finally, if you think *a picture is worth a thousand words,* use the *Patterns* drawing on the next page to engage your students in seeing, writing, drawing, or just thinking about patterns in a different way. The activities that accompany this drawing should work wonders for those students who delight in making meaning of patterns through color, shape, form, and design.

Activity 8

Content: Math

Lesson: Comparing

Standard: Students will recognize that patterns can emerge from real-world situations.

Multiple Intelligences: Visual/Spatial: Students will look at a drawing. Students will draw. Logical/Mathematical: Students will make comparisons.

Materials: Copies of the patterns drawing

Grade Level: K

Objective: Students will draw a picture of what they eat for breakfast and compare real-world patterns found in that drawing to the patterns found in the Patterns drawing.

Before: Students will review patterns by looking around their own homes for real-world patterns.

First: Students will draw a picture of what they eat for breakfast.

Next: Students will use the patterns drawing in this chapter and compare it to their own picture of breakfast.

Then: Students will discuss various patterns found in the two drawings.

Finally: Students will reflect upon other patterns found in the kitchen, bedroom, garage, or bathroom of their own homes.

Alternative Assessment: None

Activity 9

Content: Math

Lesson: Counting

Standard: Students will use manipulatives to count, order, and group.

Multiple Intelligences: Visual/Spatial: Students will use visual stimuli. Logical/Mathematical: Students will count objects.

Materials: Copies of patterns drawing

Grade Level: K

Objective: Students will count and categorize different patterns.

Before: Students will count various things in the classroom, such as children, desks, windows, coats, and so on.

First: Students will use the patterns drawing to count the different patterns in the drawing.

Next: Students will use plastic or foam shapes to re-create the different patterns found in the drawing.

Then: Students will create a chart of familiar pattern shapes found in the patterns drawing.

Finally: Students will look on their own clothing to find similar patterns seen in the patterns drawing.

Alternative Assessment: None

Activity 10

Content: Language Arts

Lesson: Creative Writing

Standard: Students will relate a narrative, creative story or other communication by drawing, telling, and writing.

Multiple Intelligences: Visual/Spatial: Students will draw. Logical/Mathematical: Students will problem solve. Verbal/Linguistic: Students will write.

Materials: Copies of patterns drawing

Grade Level: 2–3

Objective: Students will write a story from an existing drawing.

Before: Students will draw three or four new objects or items to add to a copy of the patterns drawing.

First: Students will look at the patterns drawing and brainstorm what each of the objects in the drawing might say if they could talk. For example:

> Egg: "I always try to be sunny in the morning."
> Butter: "I ooze all over this waffle."
> Salt Shaker: "Be careful when you shake me."
> Plate: "Round and round I go."

Next: Students will write a story or paragraph from the point of view of one of the newly added objects or items drawn onto the patterns drawing.

Then: Students will read their stories while others guess what object is speaking.

Finally: The class will create a breakfast mural and write point of view sentences for each object or item drawn on the mural.

Alternative Assessment: None

Activity 11

Content: Language Arts

Lesson: Telling Stories

Standard: Students will use effective vocabulary and organization to relate information.

Multiple Intelligences: Visual/Spatial: Students will use the patterns drawing as a stimulus for telling a story. Verbal/Linguistic: Students will tell a story. Intrapersonal: Students will reflect upon past experiences.

Materials: Copies of the patterns drawing

Grade Level: K–3

Objective: Students will look at the drawing in this chapter and tell an original story.

Before: Students will review important aspects of telling a story.

First: Students will use the patterns drawing as a stimulus for telling stories about animals or humans who might connect in some way to the scene in the picture.

Next: Students will relate personal stories that correspond to the original stories being told.

Then: Students will answer "What would happen if . . ." questions about the picture.

Finally: Students will reflect upon their own appreciation of the drawing.

Alternative Assessment: Students will take the patterns drawing home and ask a family member to tell them a story that comes from viewing the drawing.

To wrap up this chapter, here is every idea you ever wanted to know about patterns. Maybe you will begin each day helping the children find a hidden pattern in the classroom.

Patterns K–3

V/L	Read several patterned children's picture books. Discuss.	Make verbal distinctions among the different patterns.	Discuss similarities, differences, and purposes for natural patterns in artichokes, pineapples, and pinecones.	Write a poem about the pattern connections among the three.	Select one of nature's patterns. Write or give an oral report.
L/M	Use wood blocks to create specific patterns that solve a problem.	Count the shell chambers.	Create a chart for clarification.	Take a walk around the school. Deduct or infer how patterns observed were created.	Compare vein patterns in leaves with those in your body.
V/S	Duplicate the patterns using colored manipulatives on the overhead.	Look for patterns in other parts of the school such as the lunchroom, playground, and so on.	Bring different flowers to school.	Classify seashells. Look for spiral patterns.	Find patterns in hybrid corncobs. Relate these patterns to other patterns.
B/K	Duplicate the patterns with manipulatives.	Use the computer to create a page of patterns.	Move the body in four connected movement patterns.	Take a field trip to a nursery. Look for patterns in plants, rocks, and tiles.	Create a dance from the patterns found on the corncobs.
M/R	Select appropriate music. Discuss patterns found in the selections.	Use percussion instruments to create musical patterns.	Create a patterned hand-jive or chant.	Use the rhythm section of a synthesizer to assist students in creating a rhythm pattern.	Sing a simple song. Find its patterns. Hum it, tap it, la-la it, and think it.
Inter	In pairs, teach the class about patterns found in certain fruit and why they are found there.	Lead a group discussion on personal everyday patterns at home.	Collaborate on creating breakfast, lunch, or dinner patterns found at home.	Teach a lesson on weather patterns.	Volunteer to bring in different foodstuffs for this experience.
Intra	"If the inside of an apple looks like a star, the inside of a star might look like an _____ because _____."	Create a pattern with three colors of clay. Reflect upon its meaning.	Think about all the things you do on a weekend. Are there patterns in those events?	"What patterns in the classroom are the most pleasing to you?"	Use one of the foods to complete this sentence: "Patterns in this _____ remind me of _____."
N	Investigate why a shell is a perfect example of a pattern for certain animals.	Look at bark trees. Compare. Research why trees have bark.	Spend time observing patterns on the wings of butterflies.	Research patterns on snakes and their purposes.	Animals have patterns of behavior. Discover some in your own pets.

The activities and experiences in this grid are just a bit more difficult and can bring some challenges to your students. These ideas can be used as extension lessons or individual projects, or, in some cases, in learning centers.

Patterns 4–6

V/L	Make a list of spirals and curves that you see as you walk home from school.	Write a nature myth of "how the daisy got its petals."	Create analogies using pinecones or another of nature's patterns.	Write a poem using locomotor patterns as onomatopoeia.	Bring three spiraled objects to class. Discuss their similarities and differences.
L/M	Use aerial maps or topographical maps to make inferences to land patterns.	Compare these patterns to ones seen by the naked eye.	Use slides of spiderwebs to "talk" math.	Transfer the "calls" into concrete symbols.	Find four manmade patterns that are similar to four natural patterns.
V/S	Use yarn to create spiderweb orbs.	Find orbs in nature.	Keep a weekly science sketchbook of nature's patterns.	Use a microscope to locate patterns in hair, dirt, and dust.	From magazines pictures, create a montage of nature's branchings.
B/K	Follow each other as you walk. Recreate each other's walk patterns.	Take a field trip around the school or to a park looking for nature's tendrils.	Create a board game about nature's patterns.	Use a digital camera to photograph spiderwebs.	Create movements to accompany the rap.
M/R	Re-create this patterned walk to rhythmic beats.	Collect bird calls on tape.	Tape each other speaking. Listen to the different patterns of speech.	Find the perfect music as a soundtrack for your presentation.	Use the list of nature's patterns found in this chapter to create a rap or song.
Inter	Create a community bulletin board using yarn webs and fact "pockets."	Role-play or debate the significance of patterns in our daily lives.	In pairs, create a verbal/visual fact book about one of nature's patterns.	Show and tell the class about your spiderwebs.	Put together a group science display from the information.
Intra	"How do patterns improve your life?" Draw or write your answer.	Find rock patterns. Reflect upon how they are "like your class."	Define a "crag" without using words.	Use toothpicks to define a "whorl." Write a journal entry about the visual representation.	Write a reflective piece about this montage.
N	Investigate the nature of bird calls.	Show evidence of wind and water in the formation of some of nature's patterns.	Discover natural and architectural examples of meanderings.	Demonstrate logical reasons for patterns found in architecture.	Research fractals in nature. Look for evidence in and around your own home.

ROCKS

Dear Teacher,

Byrd Baylor, in her exquisite and timeless children's book, *Everybody Needs a Rock* (New York: Atheneum, 1974), says this about rocks:

> The thing to remember about shapes is this: Any rock looks good with a
> hundred other rocks around it on a hill. But if your rock is going to be special
> it should look good by itself in the bathtub.

I continue to refer to this passage each time I teach a lesson on rocks. It simply brings to mind how personal rocks can be to each of us, especially children. My request, then, is for you to bring that personal nature into the classroom at the onset of your unit on rocks. Here's how you do it. Go to the Pier One nearest you and purchase a little bag of polished agate rocks. There are about fifty in a bag. They are beautiful, and no two are alike. Your children will love them. They will want to keep them. And they will. But first, bring the rocks to class because you will use those little rocks over and over again with the activities in this chapter.

To introduce your boys and girls to these wonderful pebbles, fill up a clear glass or plastic container of water and place a few of the rocks in at a time. The transformation is amazing. All of the colors and nuances of the rocks are immediately recognizable. The rocks come alive in the water. Next, sit around the container with your kids and have a wonderful conversation about what you see. That is all. Just let the kids talk about what the rocks look like to them, what the colors represent as well as the shapes and the combination of rocks that are in the bottom of the container. Lead them with questions such as:

1. What does this particular rock remind you of?
2. If this were another object beside a rock, what could it be?
3. Select three of your favorite rocks and show me some similarities in those three rocks.
4. Complete this sentence: "If I could give this rock as a gift to someone, that someone would be _____, because _____."
5. Tell me how you think this rock got its unique design.
6. This rock is the most beautiful of all of them because _____.
7. When I hold this rock in my hand, it feels like _____.
8. Why does everybody need a rock?
9. Choose one word that best describes each of these rocks.
10. Pick two rocks that look the most different. Tell me why they are so dissimilar.

Then ask the boys and girls to select a rock to which they have been drawn the most. Distribute the favorite rocks to the children. Each child will keep the rock for a week, and as the week goes by, each child will make journal entries or answer teacher-directed reflective questions at the end of each day. Sample daily reflective questions may be:

Monday: How did you explain the rock to the rest of your family?

Tuesday: Tell me one adventure your rock has been on since you have had it.

Wednesday: If rocks had feelings or emotions, what would your rock's feeling or emotion be right now?

Thursday: If your rock could speak, tell me what it would say right now.

Friday: What has been the most difficult thing about carrying a rock around with you for one week?

There is one more thing I would like for you to do before we begin this chapter of rock activities. Give students a piece of art paper and have them draw the rock they have chosen. Focus on detail, shape, and color but not necessarily on size. They may wish to enlarge the drawing so as better to see the design of the rock. Now students will use this art piece as a collector of descriptive words about the rock as the rock goes through the week. At the beginning of each day, students will remember the events of the night before and write descriptive words on the art paper that relate to the rock the previous day or night. Some may wish to write down the descriptive words at the end of each school day and at the beginning of the following day. By the end of the week, the students should have a healthy supply of descriptive words, which will be used in one of the activities in this chapter.

Let us end the introduction to this chapter with a quote from another memorable classic by Byrd Baylor, *The Other Way to Listen* (New York: Charles Scribner's Sons, 1978). This particular quote is a gentle reminder that with the limitless avenues we have of teaching all about rocks, there is an important element of coexistence with the geology of this planet that is important for children to know.

We saw the lizard sunning on the rock. Of course, we stopped. The old man said, "I wonder how that lizard feels about the rock it's sitting on and how the rock feels about the lizard?"

See what I mean? Now it is time for you to head to the store and get that little bag of teachable moments.

You remember the first time you saw the Grand Canyon. It was in winter, in fact, and you drove past the entrance, through the thick pines and brush, wondering if you were in the right place. There were no signs whatsoever of the big hole in the ground, and you thought that perhaps you were in the wrong state.

As your dad followed the other cars down the narrow road, your 12-year-old enthusiasm kicked into overdrive. "Are we there yet?" you asked enough times to cause the vein in your mom's neck to play a rendition of a John Philip Sousa melody. Suddenly your dad's big old tank of a Chrysler rounded a slight curve and there it was, the canyon. You still remember the feeling, after all these years.

And you understood, for the first time, the true definition of awe, even for a 12-year-old kid. Many years later, you listened to Aaron Copland's Grand Canyon Suite, *and the feeling of awe returned and settled next to the same feeling of so many years before. And in an instant you had the makings of a brilliant lesson on rocks. A teachable moment had eroded itself into your life, and you were ever so pleased.*

Activity 1

Content: Language Arts

Lesson: Descriptive Words

Standard: Students will interpret visual clues that enhance the comprehension of text.

Multiple Intelligences: Visual/Spatial: Students will observe the physical characteristics of polished agates. Verbal/Linguistic: Students will give verbal clues as to the identity of specific rocks.

Materials: Polished rocks

Grade Level: K–3

Objective: Students will play "I Spy" using descriptive words as clues.

Before: Polished agates that belong to the students will be placed on a table in the room. Students will get a chance to look at the rocks and make notes about the different characteristics of the rocks.

First: The teacher will lead off by selecting a rock that is on the table and giving visual clues to its identity. Children will listen to the clues and try to guess what rock the teacher is describing.

Next: Students will take turns playing I Spy with each other's rocks, giving visual clues also as to the identity of the rocks.

Then: Students will sit in a circle and discuss the different visual clues that were given, such as shape, color, size, similarities, differences, and so on. Students will then walk outside and play the game with natural rocks found near the school or on the playground.

Finally: Students will think about or reflect upon the power of color and design when describing something in nature.

Alternative Assessment: Students will bring in one rock from outside and tell everything they know about that rock.

Activity 2

Content: Science

Lesson: Writing a Report

Standard: Students will plan and present a report using two or more visual media.

Multiple Intelligences: Verbal/Linguistic: Students will speak and read. Visual/Spatial: Students will draw.

Materials: Art paper, sample rocks, bulletin board

Grade Level: 3

Objective: Students will select a particular kind of rock and write a report and illustrate the report.

Before: Review various rocks and minerals such as rocks on the seashore, igneous rocks, volcanic rocks, sedimentary rocks, limestone caves, metamorphic rocks, marble, flint, fossils, and so on.

First: Students will select one type of rock or mineral on which to write a report and will illustrate the report.

Next: Students will display the illustrated aspect of the report on a rock bulletin board. Each illustration of selected rock types will be placed on the bulletin board with an accompanying sentence that gives one fact about that particular rock or mineral. A table display of similar rock samples will be available for the children to allude to, as well, when giving their reports.

Then: Students will give reports to the class and share their particular illustrations on the bulletin board.

Finally: Students will reflect upon anything "unique" that was discovered about rocks in their research endeavors.

Alternative Assessment: Teacher will use the bulletin board as a review tool.

Activity 3

Content: Science

Lesson: Rock Jigsaw Puzzles

Standard: Students will describe basic Earth materials.

Multiple Intelligences: Bodily/Kinesthetic: Students will take photos of rock displays or pictures of rocks in resource books. Logical/Mathematical: Students will solve a problem.

Materials: Camera, magazine, or book pictures of rock collections; heavy cardboard

Grade Level: 2–3

Objective: Students will put together a jigsaw puzzle of rock pictures.

Before: Use a digital camera to take close-up pictures of different assortments of rocks. One picture may include photos of the Grand Canyon. One picture may include volcanoes and volcanic rock. One picture may include limestone caves. One picture may include igneous rocks. There are other choices as well, including metamorphic rocks, sedimentary rocks, eroded rocks, coal, flint rocks, and so on. Once the pictures are taken, mount them onto a heavy piece of cardboard and cut the mounted picture into jigsaw-like pieces. Place the pieces into a large envelope.

First: Students will select any jigsaw puzzle to solve. Once the puzzle has been completed, students will compare it to pictures and information on rocks found on the bulletin board.

Next: Students may wish to take the digital camera outside, take a landscape picture that includes a rock or rocks, and create their own jigsaw puzzle of that particular picture. This picture will be placed in an envelope as well.

Then: Students try to put these kinds of puzzles together. However, the difference in this step is that they must then go outside and try to find the exact spot where the picture was taken. Students then return to the class and discuss and describe the physical space in which the rock in the picture was found.

Finally: Students will respond to this reflective question: "How do you think the rock in the landscape jigsaw puzzle got there?"

Alternative Assessment: Use landscape jigsaw puzzles as review tools.

Activity 4

Content: Science, Language Arts

Lesson: Rock Hunt

Standard: Students will describe basic Earth materials. Students will write a personal narrative or original story.

Multiple Intelligences: Bodily/Kinesthetic: Students will look for particular rocks. Verbal/Linguistic: Students will write a story.

Materials: None

Grade Level: 2–3

Objective: Students will go on a scavenger hunt, look for particular rocks, and write a paragraph about one of the rocks.

Before: Make copies of the following list, "The Ten Best Things about Rocks."

The Ten Best Things about Rocks

    1. A rock can be smooth.

    2. A rock can be teeny-tiny.

3. A rock can look like a heart.

4. A rock can look like a piece of candy.

5. A rock can have holes in it.

6. A rock can look like it's smiling.

7. A rock can be warm.

8. A rock can look like a face.

9. A rock can have bumps.

10. A rock can look very strange.

First: Give each student a copy of "The Ten Best Things about Rocks." Take them outside. Each student will carry a paper or plastic bag. Using the "Ten Best Things" list as a guide, students will go on a rock hunt and collect rocks that fit those criteria.

Next: Students will bring the rocks inside and categorize them, as a class, according to the "Ten Best Things" list.

Then: Students will discuss their findings.

Finally: Read the "ten best" section of Bernard Waber's wonderful old children's book, *Nobody Is Perfect* (Boston: Houghton-Mifflin, 1971). Students will reflect upon keeping their own personal ten best lists, such as the ten best pets to have, ten best vacation spots, ten best baseball cards, ten best dolls, ten best bicycles, ten best friends, and so on. Each will create a personal ten best list and work on it for a week.

Alternative Assessment: Students may wish to write a paragraph about a certain rock that has a definite connection to one of the characteristics on "The Ten Best Things about Rocks" sheet.

Activity 5

Content: Language Arts, Math

Lesson: Reflection, Problem Solving

Standard: Students will make statements of logic.

Multiple Intelligences: Logical/Mathematical: Students will problem solve. Verbal/Linguistic: Students will write.

Materials: Rocks

Grade Level: 3+

Objective: Students will make logical or illogical statements. Students will reflect upon the answers.

Before: Hold a rock up before the class and make this statement: "This rock can be used to build a dam, but it can't be used to build a boat."

First: Students will select a rock and create similar illogical and logical statements about the rock. The first statement must be factual. The second must be illogical. Both statements must have some connection. Suggested statements to stimulate the students are:

1. This rock can be used for home plate, but it can't be used as a baseball.
2. This rock can be used to sit on, but it can't be used as a cushion.
3. This rock can be used instead of grass in the yard, but it can't be used as a tree.
4. This rock can be used as sand at the beach, but it can't be used as driftwood.
5. This rock can be used to fry an egg, but it can't be used to fry chicken.

Next: Students will discuss logical and illogical reasoning.

Then: Students will transfer the discussion from rocks to daily logical and illogical situations that occur in the classroom.

Finally: Students will draw a picture showing one illogical place to find a rock.

Alternative Assessment: Students will share each other's drawings and make inferences.

Activity 6

Content: Science

Lesson: Environmental Designs

Standard: Students will construct "habitats" that illustrate simple concepts and compare them to what they represent.

Multiple Intelligences: Visual/Spatial: Students will draw a picture. Students will look at diverse natural environments. Logical/Mathematical: Students will research and fact find.

Materials: Rocks, art paper or cardboard sheets, crayons or markers

Grade Level: 2–3

Objective: Students will create an environmental design for a rock and label five facts about the environment in which the rock is placed.

Before: Lead a discussion on why and how certain rocks "fit" in certain geographic/geological areas. Show pictures of various geologic settings, such as lava flows, volcanoes, national parks, seashores, streams, caves, and coal mines, which support the diverse geology of certain areas.

First: Students will select a rock and create an environmental design in which the rock will be placed. Students may use crayons or watercolors, art paper, or cardboard sheets.

Next: When the environmental design is completed, students will research and label and/or write four or five factual statements on the environmental picture.

Then: Students will share the designs and facts with the rest of the class. Students will compare their environmental pieces to the pictures that were presented by the teacher at the beginning of the lesson.

Finally: Students will reflect upon their environmental designs by answering this question: "My rock fits in my environment because _____."

Alternative Assessment: Use these designs as review tools.

Activity 7

Content: Language Arts

Lesson: Point of View

Standard: Students will use correct conventions: spelling, punctuation, grammar, word usage, and penmanship.

Multiple Intelligence: Verbal/Linguistic: Students will write a story.

Materials: Rocks

Grade Level: 3

Objective: Students will use a rock as a catalyst for writing point of view paragraphs or stories.

Before: Hold up a rock and read some point of view stories to the class, such as the ones below.

    a. First-Person: It was a bright sunny Saturday afternoon. There I was, sitting under a big shady apple tree. There wasn't much happening that day. I could see a little league game going on across the way. Suddenly, the ball was hit toward me. A little girl about 4 or 5 years old ran up to me. She was supposed to pick up the ball, but instead she picked me up. I was scared at first. I am so sick of kids throwing me around or kicking me around. But this time was different. The little girl picked me up and dusted me off and ran her fingers all over me. I was tickled at first, and then it felt nice. She gave me a little kiss and put me in her pocket. She called me her friend and started talking to me all the way back to the baseball stands, where her parents were waiting for her.

        She called me her friend and began talking to me as she and her parents drove home. That night, I was cleaned in a nice warm bubble bath and placed in a pretty jewelry box, where I fell asleep and dreamed beautiful dreams all night long.

    b. Second-Person: You know you are loved when you are squeezed, held up to the sun, and taken on a journey. You know you are magic when you are given to a friend.

    c. Third-Person: He looked across the river and saw something glimmering. This magical light caught his eye. What could it be? Was it a message in a bottle showing him where to find a hidden chest of rubies? Could it be a diamond ring that was lost years ago and happened to wash up on this very spot? Was it a priceless treasure that would make his life perfect? He saw that the river was shallow enough to cross. As he did, the glimmering object came into view. It was a priceless treasure, all right: a perfect rock waiting just for him.

First: Students will discuss the different points of view in each of these three stories. Students will use one of the agate rocks given to them by the teacher and think of one sentence each about that rock, using first-, second-, and third-person points of view.

Next: Students will write an original story or paragraph using one of the points of view.

Then: Students will place the revised and corrected stories on sheets of paper with their rocks and display them. They will invite another class to come and enjoy the rock story exhibit.

Finally: Students will reflect upon inanimate objects having the power of speech. An example of a reflective question is "If a _____ could have the power of speech, it might say _____."

Alternative Assessment: As a variation, students will write a factual point of view story about a rock. The story must include at least three facts learned about rocks.

✔ *And now, what about five good lessons from one good book?* See if these work.

The book: Dengler, Marianna. Illustrated by Sibyl Graber Gerig. (1996). *The Worry Stone*. Flagstaff, AZ: Rising Moon.

1. Students will read the story and describe their own understanding of what a worry stone is. They will have one week to find the perfect worry stone.
2. Students will take time at the end of the day or week to share how they used their worry stones during that time.
3. Students will interview grandparents about how they make themselves feel better when they are concerned over some issue or situation.
4. Students will research fetish or totem symbols of indigenous tribes.
5. Students will create a giveaway ceremony in order to give their own worry stones away to someone else in the class.

✔ *Oh yes. Remember the teachable moment* that introduced our activities in this chapter? Well, here is a little lesson to go with that idea.

Activity 8

Content: The Arts

Lesson: Music and Geology

Standards: Students will listen to musical examples with sustained attention and self-discipline. Students will explain personal preferences for a specific musical work.

Multiple Intelligences: Musical/Rhythmic: Students will listen to music and make personal connections to the music. Intrapersonal: Students will reflect upon the significance of a piece of music. Visual/Spatial: Students will look at pictures of national parks.

Materials: Aaron Copland's *Grand Canyon Suite*

Grade Level: 3

Objective: Students will use music as a reflective tool to integrate a visual understanding of rocks and mountains to an aural understanding.

Before: Students will look at a collection of slides, transparencies, or magazine pictures of the Grand Canyon. A short lesson of its history will be given. Students will reflect upon these leading questions:

1. How was it formed?
2. What would it be like to have lived there?
3. How would you survive the winters or summers there?
4. How would you gather food and clothing?
5. How would you keep from getting lost?

6. What would be your first thought upon seeing the Grand Canyon if you were an early explorer?

7. Have you ever been to the Grand Canyon? Share that experience.

8. Upon seeing pictures of the Grand Canyon, what does it make you think of?

First: Show pictures again. This time, play specific parts of Aaron Copland's *Grand Canyon Suite*. Ask students to write down words that come to mind as they look at the pictures and listen to the music simultaneously. Ask students to look for sounds in the music that show a feeling of power, lightness, beauty, soaring, and so on.

Next: Students will discuss the feelings the music brings to them. They will listen to the music again as they draw their own version of the Grand Canyon using the music as a stimulus.

Then: Students will share their drawings. Teacher will read *G Is for Grand Canyon*, by Barbara Gowan, illustrated by Katherine Larson (Chelsea, MI: Sleeping Bear Press, 2002). Lead a discussion on this children's book using the following discussion questions and activity ideas:

1. Look at the illustrations in the book. Show signs of rocks of various kinds.

2. Re-create the Grand Canyon using long pieces of multicolored butcher paper.

3. Write reports about animals, weather, rock formations, the Colorado River, and so on. Place the reports on the replica of the Grand Canyon.

4. Use the Internet or other resources to compare the Grand Canyon to other national parts such as Glacier and Yosemite.

5. Research tribes who live or lived in the Grand Canyon.

Finally: Students will make personal connections between their drawings and the music. They will journal this question: "When I hear the song _____, I often think of _____."

Alternative Assessment: As a general reflective assessment, play several selections of different genres of music. Students will use emotion or action words to define the feelings that come from listening to the music selections.

✔ Finally, if you think *a picture is worth a thousand words,* use the *Rocks* drawing on the previous page to engage your students in seeing, writing, drawing, or just thinking about fossils, minerals, gems, mountains, caves, or other rock varieties. The activities relating to the rocks drawing should work wonders for boys and girls who love all there is to love about rocks. What better way to teach these concepts than through shape, color, form, and design?

Activity 9

Content: Language Arts

Lesson: Poetry

Standard: Students will use correct conventions: spelling, punctuation, grammar, word usage, and penmanship.

Multiple Intelligences: Verbal/Linguistic: Students will write. Visual/Spatial: Students will use art as a stimulus for writing.

Materials: Copies of rocks drawing

Grade Level: 3

Objective: Students will make a list of words that come from viewing the rocks drawing. Students will use the list of words to write a poem about the drawing.

Before: Students will color the rocks drawing and discuss what they see in the drawing.

First: Students will look at the rocks drawing and create a collective list of nouns and a list of verbs that come from the drawing. The list may include:

> Nouns: Clouds, rocks, water, shadows, vines, fish, fins, waves, boy, girl, sky, fern, whale, ocean, sea, summer
>
> Verbs: Float, climb, swim, flow, grow, lie, pile, gulp, roll, play, walk

Next: Students will use a combination of these words to write a poem about the rocks drawing. Examples to share with the class are:

> a. The water flows down from the rocks.
>   It meets the fish and helps them swim
>   Through the blue, blue water.
> b. **R**olling down the rocks
>   **O**ver the ferny vines
>   **C**alming the playful fish
>   **K**eeping the whale safe
>   **S**ummer sea.

    c. I climb the rocks
       To reach the sky
       And hear the rushing water
       Push me toward the clouds.
    d. The gurgle of water
       The cracking of rocks
       The splish-splash of fish
       The plopping of whales
       Tells me it is summer.

Then: Students will share their poems.

Finally: Students will reflect upon their own experiences by the sea.

Alternative Assessment: Students will take the rocks drawing home and create other poems with input from family members.

Activity 10

Content: Science, Social Studies

Lesson: Research

Standard: Students will describe and explain the interrelationship of populations, resources, and environments.

Multiple Intelligences: Interpersonal: Students will volunteer to gather specific information. Students will interview people. Verbal/Linguistic: Students will write a report. Visual/Spatial: Students will use art as a catalyst.

Materials: Copies of rocks drawing

Grade Level: 3

Objective: Students will give an oral report about interrelationships in an seashore setting.

Before: Students will designate the different aspects of the rocks drawing such as ocean, rocks, plants, fish, whales, humans, and clouds.

First: Students will get in groups and brainstorm interview questions about the interrelationships of these items in ocean environments (ocean, rocks, plants, fish, whales, humans, and clouds).

Next: Students will divide the questions and interview people in the community or at school who are experts on ocean/beach environmental interrelationships.

Then: The groups will bring the collective information back to class and give an oral report of their findings.

Finally: Students will reflect upon the process of working together, interviewing strangers, and giving the oral reports.

Alternative Assessment: Students will create fact cards on environmental interrelationships and keep them for further use.

Activity 11

Content: Social Studies

Lesson: Pollution

Standard: Students will identify natural and human characteristics of places and how people interact with the environment.

Multiple Intelligences: Logical/Mathematical: Students will problem solve cause-and-effect scenarios. Visual/Spatial: Students will draw. Verbal/Linguistic: Students will write. Interpersonal: Students will work together to meet some goal.

Materials: Copies of rocks drawing

Grade Level: 3

Objective: Students will draw cause-and-effect pictures of pollution, and then write a report.

Before: Students will use the rocks drawing as a guide for creating a KWL chart about pollution in oceans, on waterways, and at the beach.

First: Students will use individual copies of the rocks drawing to include in that drawing evidence of pollution. This evidence may be added drawings of haze, trash on the beach, dead fish, oil-polluted water, and so on.

Next: Students will research one aspect of pollution found on beaches and waterways.

Then: Students will give short oral or written reports of their findings, using the rocks drawing as a visual guide for the class.

Finally: Students will reflect upon their own efforts of keeping waterways clean from pollution of all types.

Alternative Assessment: Students will use copies of the rocks drawing to add more original drawings showing evidence of clean air, clean water, and clean environment.

Activity 12

Content: Language Arts

Lesson: Creative Writing, Point of View

Standard: Students will use the writing process to complete a variety of writing tasks. Students will write an original story.

Multiple Intelligence: Verbal/Linguistic: Students will write a story.

Materials: Copies of rocks drawing

Grade Level: 3

Objective: The students will use the rocks drawing as a catalyst for writing an original story about a vacation at the beach.

Before: Lead the students into a discussion about vacations at the beach. Ask the class to bring pictures, seashells, rocks, or any evidence of seaside vacations. Share those artifacts.

First: Students may use any point of view to write an original story about their own vacation experiences, or they may create an original fictitious story using the rocks drawing as their setting.

Next: Students will pair up. One student will read his story while the other student draws what she hears, creating an illustration for her partner's story.

Then: The stories and the illustrations will be collected and bound into a class book.

Finally: Students will reflect upon this question: "The best vacation I ever had was _____ because _____."

Alternative Assessment: None

Activity 13

Content: Arts, Math, Science

Lesson: Three-Dimensional Representations

Standard: Students will demonstrate a knowledge and use of a variety of techniques to create a three-dimensional project.

Multiple Intelligences: Verbal/Linguistic: Students will write reports or original stories. Logical/Mathematical: Students will use math skills.

Materials: Copies of rocks drawing, aquarium, rocks, plastic fish, pipe cleaners, additional art supplies

Grade Level: 2–3

Objective: Students will recreate the rocks drawing as a three-dimensional project.

Before: Students will write and print a flyer/newsletter about the desire to build an ocean scene in an aquarium. The flyer/newsletter will be sent to parents addressing the need for donated supplies.

First: Students will use math skills to construct the replica of the rocks drawing in a watertight container such as a terrarium, aquarium, or large clear plastic tub.

Next: Students will use this physical setting as a stimulus for various writing or problem-solving scenarios. Suggested ideas include:

1. Creative writing
2. *If* and *then* scenarios
3. "I wonder..." scenarios
4. Measurement
5. Estimation
6. Oral reports

7. Myths
8. Research
9. Literature
10. Drama activities
11. Visual art activities
12. Music activities
13. Ongoing science explorations
14. Personal interactions
15. Reflections

Then: Students may invite other classrooms to look at the replica and create their own lessons and projects stemming from the replica.

Finally: Students will keep a journal of their own interactions with the replica.

Alternative Assessment: Students will create a culmination piece (writing, drawing, acting, and so on) representing knowledge gained from this experience.

Activity 14

Content: Language Arts

Lesson: Telling Stories

Standard: Students will use effective vocabulary and organization to relate information.

Multiple Intelligences: Visual/Spatial: Students will use the rocks drawing as a stimulus for telling a story. Verbal/Linguistic: Students will tell a story. Intrapersonal: Students will reflect upon past experiences.

Materials: Copies of the rocks drawing

Grade Level: K–3

Objective: Students will look at the different elements of the drawing in this chapter and tell an original story.

Before: Students will review important aspects of telling a story.

First: Students will use the rocks drawing as a stimulus for telling stories about different experiences happening in the scenes in the picture.

Next: Students will relate personal stories that correspond to the original stories being told.

Then: Students will answer "What would happen if . . ." questions about the picture.

Finally: Students will reflect upon their own appreciation of the drawing.

Alternative Assessment: Students will take a drawing home and ask a family member to tell them a story that comes from viewing the drawing.

To wrap up this chapter, here is every idea you ever wanted to know about rocks. Perhaps it is time to bring back the old pet rock idea of long ago.

Rocks K–3

V/L	Show several children's books on rocks. Students will discuss favorite rocks.	"Read" local topographical maps.	Research games in which rocks are used.	Create your own descriptive words of what you see.	Write an original story of your visual discovery.
L/M	Compare the illustrations of these books.	Classify rocks according to size, shape, color, and so on.	Classify rocks according to their correct mineral names.	Create fact cards to accompany each drawing.	Make comparisons among several crystals. Talk math.
V/S	Look at a collection of rocks. Focus on color, shape, and texture.	Locate similar patterns in rock colors, shapes, and so on.	Look at several samples of igneous rock through a magnifying glass.	Using pictures as a guide, draw different agates.	Collect and look at pictures of the Grand Canyon.
B/K	From a list of rock vocabulary words, students will act or draw the definitions.	Look for rocks with certain characteristics.	Construct and decorate a rock container from an egg carton.	Make up a game using rocks and rock facts.	Explain weather and erosion using your body and pantomime.
M/R	Teach the students the song, "Big Rock" Candy Mountain.	Create a chant using facts about fool's gold.	Write two-line rhymes using information from these characteristics.	Use volcano facts to create a song about volcanos.	Create rhythmic beats to accompany these rhymes.
Inter	Students report on local geologic points of interest.	Volunteer to find information about fool's gold on the Internet.	With a partner, teach a lesson on "The Taste of Different Rocks."	Teach a lesson that distinguishes fool's gold from real gold.	Teach a lesson on how illustrators "see" rocks differently.
Intra	Keep a rock for a week. Journal its journey.	Evaluate your own ability to classify rocks.	Reflect: "I am most like a rock when I _____."	Reflect: "Why does everybody need a rock?"	Write your own poem about the grandeur of the Grand Canyon.
N	Use the school ground to go on a rock scavenger hunt.	Explore local geologic oddities.	Research active volcanos around the world.	Teach the class a lesson on one active volcano.	Research fossils and what we learn from them.

The activities and experiences in this grid are just a bit more difficult and can bring some challenges to your students. These ideas can be used as extension lessions or individual projects, or in some cases, in learning centers.

Rocks 4–6

V/L	Read from the Eyewitness Books series, *Rocks and Minerals*.	Read books about the tallest mountains in the world.	Read *America's National Parks*, by Paul Schollery (New York: DK Publishers, 2001).	Look through the *Dictionary of Geological Terms* by Bates and Jackson	Use as a resource the *Rocks and Minerals* pocket book (New York: DK Publishers, 1995).
L/M	Look at rock tools. Compare five of these tools. Create your own comparison criteria.	Create organized fact sheets of each.	Create a mileage wheel of distances from your hometown to each park.	Choose one geologic period. Write a description of that period.	Use measurement techniques to design a format for your own pocket rock book.
V/S	Create a visual guide to gemstones and birthstones by their color	Design and draw a board for a board game about a specific mountain.	Use picture montages to create a visual map of national parks.	Illustrate one aspect of your chosen period	Create illustrations for your pocket rock book.
B/K	As a class, take a field trip to a river bed. Use a geologist's hammer to crack open rocks and investigate.	Create a board game about a specific mountain using fact cards and drawings.	Construct a cutaway anatomy of a glacier.	Take a field trip to a science museum to gather more info about geologic periods.	Construct the booklet.
M/R	Create a factual chant on how coal is formed.	Learn the song "16 Tons" and teach it to another class.	Create a chant using geothermal phenomena such as geysers, hot springs, mudpots, and so on.	Create a rhythmic way to remember facts of your period.	Make your own rhythmic tools.
Inter	In groups, write a brochure that advertises a meteor crater or other evidence of rocks from space.	As a group, write directions for playing the board game.	Find one unique physical characteristic in national parks. Give a report of this finding.	As a whole class, use gathered facts to create a geologic period museum.	Teach others in the class how to construct the booklet.
Intra	Reflect upon attributes needed to become a geologist.	Reflect upon the process of creating the board game.	Reflect upon what "America the Beautiful" means to you.	What does "old" mean to you?	To whom will you dedicate your booklet? Why?
N	Research a typical job description of a geologist.	Research adaptability requirements when ascending tall mountains.	Research fossils in general and the Petrified Forest in particular.	Interview a geologist about your geologic period.	Create a glossary dictionary of scientific terms to accompany this book.

SHAPES

Dear Teacher,

On those days when I am not writing a book, chapter, lesson, or song about shapes, I don't give them a second thought. I never say to myself, "My, that grapefruit *is* extraordinarily round this morning." Or, "I have never noticed a piece of toast to be so exquisitely square before." No, I typically go through my days with more mindsets of "I wonder if my mortgage payment deserves to be on time this month?" or "Could it be that the E on my gas gauge actually does mean 'empty'?" or "Is this the day I fly to Chicago?"

But during those times when I actually am writing about shapes, then everything changes. I see shapes everywhere. I see them on my cats, at the end of my dog's face, on the sidewalk, in my car. I see them when I shower, when I mow my lawn, and at the park. Even at this moment, as I sit before the computer, I am surrounded by shapes. I see 102 little tiny circles grouped together to form a speaker for my Powerbook. I see forty-seven small, precise squares telling me that if I press a certain one, a Y pops up on my screen. Or if four particular ones are pressed in some order, the word "word" appears before my very eyes. Up above my computer on the wall, I see a myriad of rectangles. Each rectangle, large and small, frames photographs that are special to me: my beloved and magical Telluride, Colorado; a picture of my son Matthew at age 5, wearing his grandfather's favorite torn T-shirt; my astrological chart telling me that I should probably not get out of bed this year or next; and a photo of my parents, in their youth, at a picnic.

Now I am mesmerized by what I see. Like scales on a snake, geometric shapes are packed tightly around me, in every direction, as far as the eye can travel. This makes me want to walk around my own house and make lists. I want to make lists of all the geometric shapes I view in a simple residential dwelling. That is the calling at this moment, so lists I will make. And when I return, I imagine there will be an activity in my head. There usually is when I have too much free time.

Walking around in a particular space with something specific in mind makes the intended focus pop out in every direction. I would imagine that if I walked students to the cafeteria for lunch with nothing in mind for them to concentrate on but the walking, then walking is all that they would do. However, if I asked them to look for *green* things as they walked, then the trip would be absolutely, positively different. Sounds like another idea in the making, but let us stay on track and get back to the original thought.

So it was with this walk around my own house. I've never seen so many geometric shapes. They were really too numerous to mention without making this chapter unbearably long. The dilemma confronting me, then, was what to do with the information I collected. Basically, the walk alone could be a great activity for children, but making it a bit more constructed and constructive will serve us all better in the long run. And, since this could easily get out of hand with the infinite numbers of shapes before me, it seems reasonable for us to concentrate merely on circles, squares, and rectangles, with a few triangles thrown in for good measure. With that said, here are a few experiences children can have at home, with family, in what I call the "Family Geometric Scavenger Hunt."

a. Show a clock face to children at home. Ask them to go around the house looking for two objects, smaller and larger, which have the same round shape as the clock face.

b. Show a microwave. Children will look inside the refrigerator for objects that have the same rectangular shape as the microwave.

c. Show an egg. Children will look for similar ovate objects around the house.

d. Show children a book, a doorknob, and a door. They will point to the two objects that have similar rectangular shapes.

e. Go into a closet. Students will look at the design of clothes to find triangular shapes. They will then look in kitchen drawers for other objects that have that same shape.

f. Children will look in the living room for five round objects of descending or ascending size.

g. Children will use objects found in the home, car, or backyard to create lyrics for a song to the tune of "The Wheels on the Bus." Sample lyrics are as follows:

The pillows on the couch are square, square, square
Square, square, square,
Square, square, square
The pillows on the couch are square, square, square,
In the living room.
The plate on the table is round, round, round
Round, round, round
Round, round, round
The plate on the table is round, round, round
In the dining room.
The soap in the tub is rec-tang-le
Rec-tang-le
Rec-tang-le
The soap in the tub is rec-tang-le
In the bathroom.

h. Children will closely observe any pets in the home. Ask them to look at cat ears and find something around the house that is triangular in shape.

i. Children will use the backyard to find any of nature's objects that are rectangular, round, square, or triangular in shape. They will compare these natural shapes to manmade shapes found in the house.

The main objective to these kinds of simple activities is to offer younger children, at home or at school, ways to be more keenly aware of the environment in which they live and learn. My suggestion is to pick one type of object to observe every day or week, whether it be shapes, colors, textures, sizes, specific letters of the alphabet, particular numbers, or what have you. And when boys and girls go about their typical day, in school or at home, on vacation, or at the grocery or drug store, there is always something in the back of their mind that asks them to use that mind.

This chapter spends a majority of time with activities that require students to observe, figure out, and name. Hopefully, it will also draw together the important connection that nature's geometric shapes have with the shapes of the youngsters' other worlds.

You are having a birthday party for two of your best friends who have turned the delicious age of 50. You want this to be a special occasion, so you go to the grocery store to find just the right collection of food for this auspicious event.

As you meander through the aisles tossing items such as prunes, melba toast, vanilla pudding, and lactose-free buttermilk into your shopping cart, you head for the deli where there is a special on chipped beef. While making your way toward the counter at the back of the store, you happen to walk past the cereal section. Suddenly a wheel on your cart hits something on the floor, causing the entire cart to careen into the shelf next to you. As if ordained by a higher power, a box of Cheerios somersaults into your cart, hitting the four-pack of vanilla pudding and landing upright in your basket. You swoon at the immediate possibilities. And in an instant, you have the makings of a brilliant lesson on geometric shapes. A teachable moment has tumbled into you life, and you are ever so pleased.

Activity 1

Content: Math, Language Arts

Lesson: Activity Center

Standards: Students will follow multistep directions. Students will use techniques to facilitate computation.

Multiple Intelligences: Logical/Mathematical: Students will count objects found in a children's book. Visual/Spatial: Students will use pictures to assist in an understanding of numbers. Verbal/Linguistic: Students will read along as they listen to an audio version of a children's book.

Materials: Tape recorder, selected children's book, packet of cardboard squares (packet 1); art paper, string, cardboard diamond shapes, glue (packet 2); chart of various shapes

Grade Level: K–2

Objective: The students will listen to a taped version of a children's book and follow directions given on the tape.

Before: Make an audiotape of Dayle Ann Dodd's children's book, *The Shape of Things* (Asheville, NC: Candlewick Press, 1994).

First: Individual students will use earphones to listen to the audiotape of *The Shape of Things* and to the following directions that have also been taped for students to use in an "audio activity center." A packet of activities will be available to the students as will a hard copy of the selected book. Below is the script to be used for taping Dodd's book, *The Shape of Things*.

Taped directions:

Please open your book to the inside cover.

Now count the squares on the inside cover. Press STOP on your cassette player before you begin counting. Once you have finished counting, press START.

How many squares did you count? _____ That's right. There are forty-six squares. Very good.

Now count the circles on the inside cover. Press STOP on your cassette player before you begin counting. Once you have finished counting, press START.

How many circles did you count? _____ That's right. There are fifty-seven circles on the inside cover. Very good.

Now let us count the triangles. Ready? Press STOP while you count. How many triangles did you count? _____ Are you sure? _____ You are right. There are only fifteen triangles on the inside cover.

It is time to read our book, so please turn to the title page. Look carefully at the title page. Do you see a group of circles? _____ Put your finger on the group of circles. _____ Now find two green triangles. _____ Put one finger on each of the two green triangles. _____ Very, very good. Find a big diamond. _____ Put your finger on that diamond. _____ Very nice job.

Please turn the page. We are ready to begin reading this book *The Shape of Things.*

(Students will follow along as they listen to the taped words on this page and then listen to the directions for this page.)

Look at the next page. _____ A house made of squares.

Can you create another picture out of squares? Pick eight squares out of the SQUARES packet and design a picture right now. Press STOP as you begin. When you finish, press START.

What is your picture? _____ Very good. Please turn the page.

(Students will follow along as they listen to the taped words on this page and then listen to the directions for this page.)

Do you have any circles on your clothes? _____ On your shoes? _____ On your skin? _____ Count all of the circles you can find on your clothes and shoes and skin. Press STOP when you are ready to count the circles. Press START when you have finished.

How many circles did you find on your clothes? _____ That many? Very, very good.

Please turn the page and read along with me.

(Students will follow along as they listen to the taped words on this page and then listen to the directions for this page.)

Count the triangles on the next page. I have counted forty. See if you can find all forty triangles on the page. Press STOP while you count. Press START when you finish.

Did you find all forty? _____ Very good.

Please turn the page as we read some more.

(Students will follow along as they listen to the taped words on this page and then listen to the directions for this page.)

There are many, many rectangles on these two pages in front of you, but how many rectangles can you find in your classroom? _____ Take a pencil and paper and walk around the room looking for rectangles. Try to find ten rectangles if you can. Press STOP as you begin. Press START when you are finished.

Did you find ten rectangles? Let us name them, beginning with number 1_____. Number 2 _____. Number 3 _____. Number 4 _____. Number 5 _____. Number 6 _____. Number 7 _____. Number 8 _____. Number 9 _____. Number 10 _____.

You did it! You found ten rectangles in the room. Very, very good.

Please turn the page as we continue to read.

(Students will follow along as they listen to the taped words on this page and then listen to the directions for this page.)

I have a question for you. Why would it be better if a hen could lay square eggs instead of oval eggs? _____ Think about it. Now write your answer on a piece of paper. Or draw a picture that shows your answer. Don't forget to stop the cassette player while you write or draw.

So, why would it be better if a hen could lay square eggs instead of oval eggs?

I like that answer. And I think that if a hen could lay square eggs instead of oval eggs, the eggs would stack better.

Please turn the page and let us continue reading. We are almost finished with this book.

(Students will follow along as they listen to the taped words on this page and then listen to the directions for this page.)

For this next activity, you will need a piece of art paper, a bunch of cut-out diamond shapes, a piece of string, and some glue. Look in packet 2 and you will find these items. When you have all of these materials, take your time and create your very own kite. Paste your kite design right onto the art paper. Press STOP on the cassette player right now. When you have finished making your kite picture, press START.

What a great kite picture. What a great kite. Now give your kite picture to a friend and ask that friend to write a poem about the kite. When your friend has written the poem, ask your friend to read the poem to you. Press STOP right now. Press START when you are ready to continue.

Please turn the page. The end of the book is almost here.

(Students will follow along as they listen to the taped words on the last two pages of the book and then listen to the directions for the last two pages.)

Look at the shape chart that is at this activity center. See if you can find any shapes on these two pages that haven't been added to the shape chart. Use a pencil to write and draw the shapes you have discovered. Please press STOP as you find new shapes and write them on the shape chart. Press START when you are ready to listen once again.

Well, boys and girls, you have completed the book, *The Shape of Things*, and all of the activities that go along with it. I hope you enjoyed reading along with me.

Before you go, however, there is one more activity for you to do. Right now, think of one shape. It could be a square, a circle, a diamond, a triangle, or a rectangle. Choose one shape. When you go home today from school, write down all the many things you see on your way home that have the same shape as you have chosen. When you come back to school tomorrow, tell the class about the most interesting thing you saw that was that shape.

Time is up. The book is done. Thank you for working so nicely. Have a nice day.

(Students will turn off the tape recorder, collect all of the activity materials, and place them in a folder or manila envelope. The envelope or folder will be placed on a shelf ready for the next student who wishes to work at this book talk activity center.)

Next: Students will share their work with others or the teacher.

Then: Students may wish to select their own children's book, record it, and, with the help of older students, create activities that might accompany the book.

Finally: Students reflect, through discussion, ways in which hearing a book and reading along with the audiotape help them in their comprehension of the book.

Alternative Assessment: Students will use pictures from magazines to create their own seven-page shape book. Students will then create their own text of the book and record it on tape. Other students will listen to the tape and have a comprehension discussion with the teacher.

Activity 2

Content: Language Arts

Lesson: Sponge Shapes

Standard: Students will follow multistep directions. Students will respond to visual forms. Students will use sponge art to express ideas.

Multiple Intelligences: Visual/Spatial: Students will create a scene with sponge art. Verbal/Linguistic: Students will write or tell a story.

Materials: Sponges cut up in various geometric shapes, art paper, tempera paint, cups, paper towels

Grade Level: K–3

Objective: Students will listen to a story and create a scene about that story using sponge art. Students will write or tell a story using a sponge art drawing.

Before: Gather the students around a piece of art paper. Place, one at a time, several sponge art geometric shapes on the paper. Students will discuss their different shapes, correct geometric names, and object names such as trees, mountains, and so on.

First: Read the following story to the class. Linger on the words and phrases that are italicized. These italicized words and phrases are verbal clues that will assist the students in creating a picture about the story, using geometrically shaped sponge pieces and tempera paint in cups. Give students directions on what to create using their sponge objects on the paper and when to do so. Make sure also that the large piece of art paper is placed vertically in front of the students and that the students begin their drawings at the bottom of the art paper.

The Tree Who Grew to the Moon

> In a beautiful forest, there lived three trees. *Two trees were very big and tall.* They were very happy and loved living in the forest. *One tree, however, was very, very small.* It seemed to look sad all the time. "Why can't I be as tall as you?" the little tree asked one day. The two big trees smiled at the little tree when he asked that question. They replied, *"Because you never look toward the sun."* "Why should I look toward the sun and get hot

and sweaty?" the little tree answered back. "I like it here in the shade." "But the sun will help make you grow," the two tall trees said.

The little tree grumbled for a moment and then decided to face *toward* the sun. Soon he could feel himself *growing* a teeny, tiny bit. "Wow!" he yelled. "What else can I do to make me grow?" The two tall trees pondered the question for a while and then said, "Little friend, if you take a big drink of water from the *pond* you will grow even more." "Why should I get wet and drippy?" the little tree answered back. "I like it here where it is dry." "But the water will help make you grow," the two tall trees said. So the little tree bent down and took a big, long drink from the pond. Soon he could feel himself *growing* a teeny, tiny bit more. "Wow!" he yelled. "What else can I do to make me grow?" The two tall trees pondered the question for a while and said, "Little friend, if you put some nice, rich *dirt* around your *roots* you will grow even more." "Why should I get dirty and icky?" the little tree answered back. "I like it here where it is nice and clean." "But if you use the marvelous soil and all its nutrients, you will grow even more," said the two tall trees. So the little tree piled lots of nice, rich dirt around his roots. Soon he could feel himself growing even *bigger and taller.* "Wow!" he yelled. "What else can I do to make me grow?" The two tall trees pondered the question for a while and said, "Little friend, if you breathe in the *wind* around you, you will grow even more." "Why should I let the wind mess up my leaves?" the little tree answered back. "I like it here where it is nice and unrumpled." "But the wind will help make you grow," said the two tall trees. So the little tree took a deep breath and filled his lungs with nice, clean air. "Wow!" he yelled. "I'm as *big as you are.*" And sure enough, he was.

As the days went by, the little tree continued to drink from the pond. He continued to put nice rich dirt on his roots. He continued to breathe in the air. And the little tree continued to get *taller.* And *taller.* And *taller.* Soon he was *taller* than the other trees. Soon he was *taller* than the *clouds floating in the sky.* Soon he was *taller* than the *two birds* flying above the clouds. Soon he was *taller* than the *building by the edge of the forest.* And soon was even taller than *the jet plane flying high above the clouds and the birds.* He even looked to be taller than the sun.

When the two tall trees realized how big and tall the little tree was growing, they began to worry about their friend. He was growing so tall that they could not see the top of his branches anymore. "Hey, up there!" they yelled. "You had better stop looking at the sun, and you had better stop drinking from the pond, and you had better stop putting dirt on your roots, and you had better stop breathing in the wind." They could hear the little tree laughing way up in the sky. "And what will happen to me if I don't?" he hollered down. "Then you will surely hit the *moon*," the two tall trees screamed back, their voices filled with dread.

And that is just what happened. The little tree grew and grew. He grew until, with a loud thud that sounded like thunder, he reached the moon. The two tall trees were saddened to see their little friend grow completely out of sight. They knew they would miss him very much.

But they needn't worry. Because on certain nights when the two tall trees look up into the sky and see only part of the moon showing, it is because the other part is covered with the sun-drenched, pond-watered, earth-covered, wind-filled branches of the little tree. And do you know what? If you look up at the moon on those certain nights when only part of the moon is showing, you can see the little tree's branches covering the moon too.

Next: Students will create their own sponge art pictures.

Then: Other students will write a story to accompany those pictures.

Finally: Students will draw, write, or discuss this reflective question: "How does the little tree ever get back to Earth?"

Alternative Assessment: Students will write their own assessment questions about their sponge art pictures.

Activity 3

Content: Science

Lesson: Comparisons

Standard: Students will identify the basic structures of plants.

Multiple Intelligences: Visual/Spatial: Students will observe shape, form, and design in nature.

Materials: Chart paper

Grade Level: K–3

Objective: Students will take a field trip outdoors and compare natural geometric shapes with man-made geometric shapes seen around the school building or in the classroom.

Before: Students will look around the room and locate manmade objects of certain geometric shapes.

First: Students will make a list of these objects and their appropriate geometric shapes.

Next: Students will take a walking field trip around the school grounds looking for natural shapes that compare with the shapes of the manmade objects found on the lists.

Then: Students will create a tactile comparison chart of both types of geometric objects, natural and manmade.

Finally: Students will reflect upon why the shapes of natural objects work best in the environment because of their specific shapes.

Alternative Assessment: Take the students back outside. As they walk around the school, point to certain objects, natural and manmade. Students will call out the appropriate geometric shape.

Activity 4

Content: Math

Lesson: Geometric I Spy

Standard: Students will recognize geometric shapes. Students will predict how combining or dividing can change shapes.

Multiple Intelligences: Logical/Mathematical: Students will recognize geometric shapes from a design sheet. Visual/Spatial: Students will create a geometric design sheet.

Materials: Computer, ruler

Grade Level: 3

Objective: Students will use computers, rulers, and so on to create a sheet of geometric designs.

Before: Review geometric shapes and their common names as well as their correct names. Put the following words on the board and have students differentiate and locate as many shapes as can be found in the room: triangle (three-sided), quadrilateral (four-sided), pentagon (five-sided), hexagon (six-sided), heptagon (seven-sided), octagon (eight-sided), nonagon (nine-sided), decagon (ten-sided), undecagon (eleven-sided), and dodecagon (twelve-sided).

First: Using J. Bourgoin's *Arabic Geometrical Pattern and Design Art Workbook* (New York: Dover Publications, 1973), which can be found in good art supply stores, or using other geometric patterned sheets from similar books, make an overhead transparency of one of the design sheets. Students will try to locate the different geometric shapes discussed above.

Next: Students will use the computer and the Appleworks program, if possible, to design and create their own geometric design sheet, incorporating as many of the shapes mentioned above as possible.

Then: Students will color the design sheet in ways to create color patterns. These sheets will be placed on the bulletin board for future discussion.

Finally: Students will think up their own "What do you think would happen?" questions about geometric shapes. For example, lead off the discussion with this question: "What do you think might be different if this book were round instead of a quadrilateral?"

Alternative Assessment: Students will cut out geometric shapes. Hold up these shapes. Students will call out the correct geometric name for the different shapes. Students will put different geometric shapes together to form a common object.

Activity 5

Content: Language Arts, Math

Lesson: Storytelling with Geometric Shapes

Standard: Students will use effective vocabulary and organization to relate information.

Multiple Intelligences: Verbal/Linguistic: Students will tell a story. Visual/Spatial: Students will recognize geometric shapes.

Materials: Cardboard cutouts of various geometric shapes.

Grade Level: K–3

Objective: Students will tell an original story using cardboard geometric shapes and a combination of those shapes as visual clues.

Before: Show a cardboard cutout of a circle and a triangle. Create an ice cream cone from those two shapes. Ask students to make a sentence using the combined shapes as a visual context clue. Ask students to ask a question using the same combined shapes as a clue. Ask students "What if . . ." questions using the combined two shapes as a visual context clue.

First: Students will practice with each other making objects from two combined geometric shaped cardboard cuts. They will make appropriate sentences using those combined shapes as visual context clues.

Next: Using a corkboard or bulletin board, place a selection of combined shapes on the board. Students will tell a story from those clues.

Then: Students will be given a packet of cardboard geometric shapes. Individually at their desks, they will create a recognizable shape or shapes and write their own paragraphs or stories about that shape.

Finally: Select one shape. Students will draw that shape on a piece of paper. They will answer this reflective statement: "If I were a _____ (quadrilateral, for example), I would be a _____. Then I could _____."

Alternative Assessment: Put a cut-out quadrilateral shape on the board. Tear one end off. Ask students to write a paragraph about how the quadrilateral can acquire a new missing end, or ask them to write a paragraph about how the end disappeared.

Activity 6

Content: Language Arts

Lesson: Sound-Movement Story

Standard: Students will prepare and deliver information to an audience.

Multiple Intelligences: Verbal/Linguistic and Bodily/Kinesthetic: Students will present a choral reading piece.

Materials: Scripts, flannel board, cut-out cardboard geometric shapes

Grade Level: 2–3

Objective: Students will read a sound-movement rendition of the story, "The Tree Who Grew to the Moon." Students will act out the story. Students will create a flannel board scene of the story.

Before: Rewrite the sponge art story, "The Tree Who Grew to the Moon," found at the beginning of this chapter, into a choral reading, sound-movement experience. Ask students to read the script. Lead discussions on appropriate movement sequences that can accompany this sound-movement idea. Students will get into groups of 3 or 4. Each group will become one of the characters in the story. Each group will be responsible for an appropriate phrase their character might say and an appropriate movement that their character might use as they say the phrase. As a narrator reads the story aloud, each time a character's name is said, that character group says the phrase attributed to them and makes the movement that has been created for their character. Also, as the narrator reads the story, the story builder places appropriate flannel cutouts on a flannel board that is situated in front of the class, near the character groups. Flannel board cutouts include two tall trees, a little tree, a pond, brown dirt, the sun, clouds, birds, wind, the moon, a jet, a building, and green and brown cutouts representing the "growth" of the little tree.

Narrator requirements, story builder requirements, and character group phrases and movements are as follows:

Narrator: Reads the story and stops each time one of the following character names is mentioned in the story. When the narrator stops, the appropriate character group acts out a movement and phrase.

Story Builder: Places flannel cutouts on the flannel board.

Little Tree: "Shake a little leaf, shake a little limb, one of these days I'll be taller than them." (Shake body vigorously.)

Two Tall Trees: "Tall and majestic are we. Tee, hee, hee, hee, hee."(Bow and curtsy. Cough as they bow.)

Sun: "I'm hotter than an egg frying on the sidewalk." (Make a wiggly movement. Make a sizzle sound.)

Pond: "Anybody got a straw?" (Make a guzzling sound.)

Dirt: "Yo! Where's a broom?" (Make a swish, swish sound.)

Wind: "Hold onto your hats, I feel a breeze." (Make a wind sound.)

Clouds: "Peek-a-boo. I see you." (Make a "wheee" sound.)

Birds: "Anybody got any goggles?" (Make a flapping sound.)

Moon: "Got any cheese?" (Make a slurping, eating sound.)

Tall Building: "Oh, no, my elevator's stuck again!" (Make a screeching sound.)

Jet Airplane: "Where's my parachute?" (Make a "zoom" sound.)

First: Each group practices their movement and phrases. Narrator practices the story. Story builder(s) practice working on the flannel board.

Next: The sound-movement story is presented.

Then: Students discuss the event and describe how comprehension of the story was increased and understood better.

Finally: Students reflect upon their abilities and understanding of the characters.

Alternative Assessment: Students may wish to think up their own original phrases and movements as the story is read again.

Activity 7

Content: Math

Lesson: Picasso and Polygons

Standard: Students will use art to express ideas and make connections. Students will predict how combining or dividing them can change shapes.

Multiple Intelligences: Visual/Spatial: Students will look at various art examples by Pablo Picasso. Logical/Mathematical: Students will make connections between Picasso's works and geometric shapes.

Materials: Art book

Grade Level: 3

Objective: Students will view selected works of art by Pablo Picasso and make connections between those works and certain geometric shapes.

Before: Collect several samples of work by Pablo Picasso, either through books, posters, or Internet sites.

First: Use the book, *Picasso*, by Ingo F. Walther (New York: Barnes and Noble Books, 2001). Show pages 36–38, 43, 59, 66, and 71, and ask the following questions relating to those pages:

> a. What do you think you see in these paintings?
>
> b. Show me a certain geometric shape.
>
> c. How does Picasso change, combine, or divide shapes?
>
> d. Count the different circles you see in these paintings.
>
> e. Show how combining or dividing these shapes has changed certain shapes.
>
> f. Find quadrilaterals in these paintings.

Next: Students will use the paintings on pages 58, 66, or 71 to create their own Picasso-esque drawings using only a combination of geometric shapes.

Then: Students will make comparisons of their paintings and those of Picasso's.

Finally: Reflect upon this question: "When do you know that a painting is finished?"

Alternative Assessment: Look at paintings other than those of Picasso, such as those of M.C. Escher. Discuss geometric shapes found in those paintings.

✔ *And now, what about five good lessons from one good book?* See if these work.

The book: Photos by Walter Wick. Riddles by Jean Marzollo. (2000). *I Spy: Extreme Challenger: A Book of Picture Riddles.* New York: Scholastic Books.

> a. On pages 10–11, find ten different shapes. Place them in alphabetical order.
>
> b. On pages 16–17, find the following quadrilateral objects: comb, candle, match, nail, and needle. Do the following with these shapes:
>
> > 1. Write rhyming words.
> >
> > 2. Describe the function of these objects.
> >
> > 3. Use each word in a complete sentence.
> >
> > 4. Look for objects on pages 18–19 that will complete the following story:

There once was a brown _____ who was very afraid of a black eight-legged _____. Every time the brown _____ saw the eight-legged _____, he would jump onto the back of the yellow _____ with the busy tail and ride away. One day the brown _____ came to a _____ crossing the road. The _____ would not get out of the road, so the brown _____ rolled a bowling _____ toward the _____ who was trying to cross the road. The _____ ran across the road and finally ran away. The brown _____ then saw a house, which was made of_____. The brown _____ unlocked the house with a special _____ and there he stayed, safe from all the eight-legged _____ that had tried to scare him.

    c. Look at pages 22–23. Find some small objects to place on your desk. Use a flashlight to create shadows from those objects. Write a story about one of the shadows that have an interesting shape.

    d. Look at the objects on pages 30–31. Find a cat, top, rabbit, playing card, and hourglass. What other shapes can you find in each one of these objects?

    e. Write a story incorporating all of these objects.

✔ *Oh yes. Remember the teachable moment* that introduced our activities in this chapter? Well, here is a little lesson to go with that idea.

Activity 8

Content: Art, Language Arts

Lesson: Cereal Pictures and Creative Writing

Standard: Students will write a personal narrative or creative story.

Multiple Intelligences: Logical/Mathematical: Students will problem solve how to create pictures out of breakfast cereal. Visual/Spatial: Students will draw a picture. Bodily/Kinesthetic: Students will construct a picture. Verbal/Linguistic: Students will write or tell an original story.

Materials: Small bags of different types of cereal with geometric shapes (Kix, Cheerios, Wheat Chex, and so on), glue, art paper

Grade Level: K–3

Objective: Students will create a picture from cereal pieces. Students will write or tell a story about the picture. The title of the story should have a geometric shape in its title. Suggested titles are:

    a. The Tree that Grew Circles

    b. A Fence of Squares

    c. The Triangle Bird that Couldn't Fly

Before: Show a model picture made from cereal. Ask students to tell a story that might accompany that particular picture. Discuss a perfect title for the picture.

First: Give students several packets of cereal of various shapes. Students will practice with the pieces before anything is glued down.

Next: Students will create original pictures using cereal pieces.

Then: Students will swap pictures and write and title a story about the picture they received. Students will read the stories to each other and show the artwork.

Finally: Students will reflect upon items or objects they use at school or home that might work better if they were, indeed, made of cereal.

Alternative Assessment: None

✔ And finally, if you think *a picture is worth a thousand words,* use the *Shapes* drawing above to engage your students in seeing, writing, drawing, or just thinking about circles, squares, triangles, and other intriguing shapes that shape our world. The activities related to the shapes drawing should work wonders for boys and girls who love shapes of all kinds. What better way to teach these concepts than through shape, of course, and color, form, and design?

Activity 9

Content: Math

Lesson: Geometric Shapes in Everyday Life, Comparisons

Standard: Students will create and expand geometric shapes.

Multiple Intelligence: Visual/Spatial: Students will identify geometric shapes.

Materials: Copies of shapes drawing

Grade Level: 2–3

Objective: The students will identify geometric shapes in the shapes drawing and draw similar geometric shapes. The students will compare their own drawings to the drawings found in a picture.

Before: Students will familiarize themselves with various geometric shapes and names by reviewing these shapes and names from geometric forms placed on the overhead.

First: Using drawing tools on the computer, a straight-edge piece of cardboard, or a ruler, students will be given a quick art lesson by the art teacher, regular classroom teacher, or another student on drawing three-dimensional shapes such as the ones in the shapes drawing.

Next: Students will look at the shapes drawing and correctly name the different geometric shapes seen in this drawing.

Then: Students will use the empty space in the shapes drawing to draw other buildings in the city formed by geometric shapes and a combination of these shapes.

Finally: Students will compare the geometric structures in both parts of the city.

Alternative Assessment: Students will compare the geometric shapes found in the shapes drawing to the shapes of structures in and around the school.

Activity 10

Content: Language Arts

Lesson: Conversational Speech, Poetry

Standard: Students will listen and respond to poetry.

Multiple Intelligence: Verbal/Linguistic: Students will listen to poetry.

Materials: Copies of shapes drawing

Grade Level: K

Objective: Students will listen to a poem and respond to the poem in relation to meaning and appreciation.

Before: Have the children look at the shapes drawing and create a spontaneous conversation between the two people in the drawing.

First: Read the following poem to the students.

> A big red balloon floated by
> With wide stripes as blue as the sky
> The girl looked around
> From a basket so brown
> And noticed the white clouds up high.
>
> She also saw something far down
> On the purple- and orange-colored ground
> It was a young man

Who was waving his hand,
And yelling, "Come visit my town."

So the girl floated, gently and slow
Toward the black and red buildings below
A flag she did see
That was green as a tree
And she said, "That is where I will go."

Now the wind caught her with a big blast
And the flag couldn't help her grab fast
So she flew right on by
Toward some birds in the sky
Who looked strangely at her as she passed.

Next: Students will listen to the poem again and use the words in the poem as context clues for coloring the shapes drawing in appropriate colors.

Then: Students will listen to the poem again to find something mentioned in the poem that is not on the shapes drawing (birds). The students will draw in the missing piece of the picture.

Finally: Students will reflect upon this question: "Riding in a hot air balloon would be fun/scary because _____." Students will also discuss their likes/dislikes of the poem itself.

Alternative Assessment: None

Activity 11

Content: Math

Lesson: Graphing

Standard: The students will create a simple graph.

Multiple Intelligence: Logical/Mathematical: Students will categorize, chart, and graph.

Materials: None

Grade Level: 2–3

Objective: Students will create a picture graph of different shapes seen in the shapes drawing.

Before: Students will look at the shapes drawing and locate various geometric shapes found in every part of the picture.

First: Students will create a simple picture graph showing these various shapes.

Next: Students will use objects found in the room to create another picture graph showing the various geometric shapes discovered there.

Then: Students will review the various shapes from the shapes drawing by pointing to each shape and calling out its appropriate name.

Finally: Students will reflect upon this question: "Living in a round house would be difficult/easy because _____."

Alternative Assessment: None

Activity 12

Content: Language Arts

Lesson: Telling Stories

Standard: Students will use effective vocabulary and organization to relate information.

Multiple Intelligences: Visual/Spatial: Students will use the shapes drawing as a stimulus for telling a story. Verbal/Linguistic: Students will tell a story. Intrapersonal: Students will reflect upon past experiences.

Materials: Copies of the shapes drawing

Grade Level: K–3

Objective: Students will look at the different elements of the drawing in this chapter and tell an original story.

Before: Students will review important aspects of telling a story.

First: Students will use the shapes drawing as a stimulus for telling stories about different experiences happening in the scenes in the picture.

Next: Students will relate personal stories that correspond to the original stories being told.

Then: Students will answer "What would happen if . . ." questions about the picture.

Finally: Students will reflect upon their own appreciation of the drawing.

Alternative Assessment: Students will take a drawing home and ask a family member to tell them a story that comes from viewing the drawing.

To wrap up this chapter, here is every idea you ever wanted to know about shapes. Maybe now is the time to round your class out with some ideas about the shape of things.

Shapes K–3

V/L	Read some children's books about shapes and try to locate them in the room.	Write a choral reading/reader's theater story about shapes.	Look for different shapes in your classroom. Discuss them.	Write a poem about your favorite shape.	Complete a supplemental worksheet on shapes.
L/M	Use scissors, paper, and a ruler to cut out various shapes.	Categorize the shapes.	Create a math problems with triangles.	Count the number of certain shapes in the room.	Use the computer to create interesting shapes.
V/S	Create a shape-of-the-week calendar.	Create a picture using a combination of geometric shapes.	Create a picture using the found objects from the scavenger hunt.	Create a clay sculpture demonstrating three shapes.	Create different shapes in a page of geometric shapes.
B/K	Use scarves or elastic bands to create various shapes.	Take a shape photographic field trip around the school.	Go on a shape scavenger hunt.	Pantomime objects that are different shapes.	Create body movements as you form shapes with scarves or elastic bands.
M/R	Sing the song, "Shapes in the Room." Create new words that have various shapes in the song.	Use photos to create a call/response chant with the shapes.	Sing "Old McDonald." Use shape names instead of animal names.	Create a rhyming poem or chant with one certain shape.	Use rhythm instruments to accompany the singing of the new "Old McDonald."
Inter	Write the rules of the shape scavenger hunt.	Read a book about shapes to another student. Teach that student something you learned.	Create written or visual task cards about shapes with a partner.	Be the leader.	With two other students, create one geometric art piece.
Intra	"My favorite shape is _____ because _____."	"If I were a circle, I would _____."	Use that shape to write or draw a personal story.	Think about how the shape of things at school or home make them work better.	Why wouldn't square wheels work on your bicycle?
N	Research shape designs on various animals, insects, and birds.	Find shapes in the architecture of your home.	Research how these designs help animals, insects, and birds survive or adapt.	Create fact cards about nature's shape.	Recreate nature's geometric shapes with the cut-out shapes.

The activities and experiences in this grid are just a bit more difficult and can bring some challenges to your students. These ideas can be used as extension lessons or individual projects, or, in some cases, in learning centers.

Shapes 4–6

V/L	Look around the classroom and have a general discussion of the different shapes observed.	Collect quotes that include the names of shapes.	Discuss shapes in relation to technology, inventions, and history.	Write a first-person story about a shape.	Write a cinquain about a certain shape.
L/M	"Talk" geometry outside.	Categorize and graph shapes found in the classroom.	Play "Guess the Object" using a combination of geometric shapes.	Explore the concept of all recreational balls being square.	Analyze why certain tools work best because of their shape.
V/S	Create a newspaper ad that sells triangle-shaped objects.	Create a design using only two shapes.	Illustrate the story.	Create your own Picasso-esque piece of art.	Look at a table of objects. Define their shapes and combinations of shapes.
B/K	Act out a puppet play in which the characters are geometric shapes.	Recreate the puppet play using students instead of puppets.	Create an exhibit of these pieces of original art.	Work with tangrams.	"Dance" shapes.
M/R	Write a chant/rap about shapes on a bicycle.	Listen to musical instruments. Discuss how shape is significant to sound.	Listen to classical music. Make inferences to "mood" and shapes.	Create sounds that define certain shapes.	Sing songs with shapes' names in the lyrics.
Inter	Brainstorm specific shapes that have "shaped" history.	Volunteer to teach younger students about shapes.	Write a puppet play with other students.	Teach that lesson.	With a partner, draw and tell a "rebus" story using shapes.
Intra	Create a collage of shapes that represent your life.	Write your own quote.	Explain why we need to know about shapes.	When do you "feel" round? Square? Rectangle?	Free write about shapes in your journal.
N	Find certain shapes in the architecture of your school. Research significance and function.	Interview builders regarding shapes and engineering aspects.	Research well-known important architectural models. Relate to shapes.	Find unusual shapes, both natural and manmade. Explain their functions.	Compare nature's shapes to technological shapes.

SNAKES AND OTHER CRAWLY THINGS

Dear Teacher,

Okay! Are you ready? Clear the classroom of all desks and tables. That's right. *All desks and tables.* Arrange your students on the floor in comfortable positions: beanbags, pillows, whatever. Now, bring *it* in. Come on. I know you can do it. Bring *it* on in. Careful! Don't tilt the glass case too much. Be very, very careful. Bring *it* on in and set it down slowly, right in the middle of the floor where all your students can see. There! You have done it. Now, step back, sit on the floor, take a whiff of smelling salts, and then ask your boys and girls to quietly observe the glass case for two minutes. No talking, no asking questions, no moving around. Just watching, watching, watching . . . the snake.

Now ask the first important question: "If you were this snake, what would you be thinking right now?" You have begun your unit on snakes and other crawly things with a reflective question. Not a bad way to begin. Follow that with a simple KWL chart. Gather all of that information about what it is the students want to know. It makes life so much simpler that way. Next, have a variety of materials and supplies scattered, in art center format, all around the room. Put out the clay, different kinds of paints, cardboard sheets, writing paper, drawing paper, aluminum foil, boxes of assorted sizes, socks, sticks, tongue depressors, magazines with pictures of snakes, and anything else you can think of that will assist in unlocking some creative expression in your boys and girls.

Then, bring in those stacks of books: children's books with bright, bold illustrations and science books with loads of information. Books related to snakes and other crawly things. No need to give out certain page numbers. The children know exactly where to look.

Finally, give your students the gift of time to make personal connections with the topic of this chapter, "Snakes and Other Crawly Things." Give them freedom to be inquisitive, to make assumptions, and to create their own vision of what a *snake* looks like to them. Put on your facilitator hat and get out of the way. Give them unrushed moments to explore and seek information, and see if it fits with what they are actually seeing in the glass cage. Give them permission to link knowledge with hearsay, myths with truths, and fears with excitement.

Give them time to find themselves in the moment, and let them dwell there. The 80+ ideas and activities in this chapter will trickle in in their own good time. Your science unit will be off to a good start because you allowed students to take ownership of their own learning right from the very beginning. It makes all the difference in the world.

When you finish that first day and have pondered how in the world to get that snake to a place in the room where *you* don't have to look at it, on your way home that afternoon, go rent *Anaconda* at the video store. Your own kids will love you for it.

You love Saturday mornings, and you love to hike. So you get up on a beautiful, mellow day, just as the sun begins its journey across the sky, and you head out through the woods behind your house. You love the rhythm the wind and the trees play for you. You like the sound of the leaves as you crunch your way along.

The path is familiar and worn, and you find that it takes you, with no effort, through and around and up and over this quiet place that looks almost like a painting. You are at peace and in your element. As you step over an old log that has been resting in that spot as long as you can remember, you scream. Not being a screamer in the global sense of the word, you are amazed at the sound that comes out of your mouth.

There, under your foot, is a snake. And you have stepped squarely on its long, slender body. You freeze, forgetting everything you instinctively know about crawly things in the wild.

Then, as your entire life passes before your eyes and you wonder who will feed the animals when you're gone, you look again and begin to laugh, a tight laugh, mind you, but a laugh, nonetheless.

For there, under your foot, isn't a snake at all, but a thin, curvy stick. You bend down and pick it up. It makes no rattling sound, so your laugh becomes a safe chuckle.

And in an instant, you have the makings of a brilliant lesson on snakes and other crawly things. A teachable moment has slithered itself into your life, and you are ever so pleased.

Activity 1

Content: Science, Creative Arts

Lesson: Snake Skin Patterns, Habitats

Standard: Students will identify basic characteristics of snakes that allow them to live in specific environments. Students will construct models that illustrate simple concepts and compare them to what they represent.

Multiple Intelligences: Verbal/Linguistic: Students will research skin patterns found in various snakes. Body/Kinesthetic: Students will create a snake and the habitat for that particular snake.

Materials: Art materials, resource books, websites

Grade Level: 2–3

Objective: The students will select and research one type of snake. The students will use found sticks to recreate the snake and its appropriate patterns. The students will build an appropriate habitat for that snake.

Before: Using The National Audubon Society's *Pocket Guide to Familiar Reptiles and Amphibians of North America* (New York: Alfred A. Knopf, 1997) or other library or online resources, students will select one type of snake on which to do research.

First: Once a snake type has been researched and information about that snake has been gathered, especially information regarding the size and physical characteristics of that particular snake, students will find a stick or tree limb or branch that best represents the size and dimension of the snake selected. The stick will be sanded down and stripped of bark if appropriate to do so. Some barks work well as scales or patterns, however.

Next: Students will paint their snake sticks in a color, design, and pattern that closely represents the actual color and pattern of the snakes they have chosen to research.

Then: Working with fifth- or sixth-grade buddies who have been researching appropriate habitats for these particular snakes, and constructing those habitats in cardboard boxes, on poster board, and so on, the primary students will join forces and bring the two aspects of this snake project together: the painted snakes and the habitats in which the snakes live.

Finally: The two grade levels will work together to write narratives that describe each habitat and type of snake. These narratives will be placed near each habitat. All of the habitats and snakes will be exhibited as a snake habitat exhibition, and the entire school will be invited to walk through and learn more about these reptiles.

Alternative Assessment: Write a joint informational newsletter to parents inviting them to the habitat exhibit. Students must contribute some bit of information about their own snakes, which will be put in the newsletter.

Activity 2

Content: Language Arts

Lesson: Patterned Poetry

Standard: Students will write a creative story or personal narrative.

Multiple Intelligences: Verbal/Linguistic: Students will write an original story. Visual/Spatial: Students will use a visual representation as a catalyst for writing a creative story.

Materials: Painted snakes, snake habitats

Grade Level: 2–3

Objective: The students will use the completed snake habitats and write a patterned poem.

Before: Read *Small Green Snake* by Libba Moore Gray, illustrated by Holly Meade (New York: Orchard Books, 1994). Point out the repetitive words and phrases used by the author to engage the reader. Make a list of those words or phrases on the board or on chart paper. The author's repetitive lines in this particular book include:

I'm a grassy grassy
garter snake
a sassy sassy
flashy flashy
tail twisting
tail turning
tail snapping
green snake
with a happy
hiss, a
hiss, a
hisssssssssss

First: Students will observe their individual or group habitats and list or discuss the descriptive words that come to mind regarding their particular snake or habitat.

Next: The teacher will model a patterned poem by using a painted snake and, with the help of the class, create a poem about that snake. For example, a representation of a rattlesnake can be used and written about. Here is a sample patterned poem about a rattler using similar word patterns found in Moore's book:

I'm a coiled, coiled
rattle snake
a flicking, flicking
scaly, scaly
rattle sounding
rattle shaking
rattle playing
rattle snake

Then: On a piece of chart paper, create the generic pattern to be used by the children:

I'm a _____, _____ (descriptive word)
_____ (name or type of snake)
a _____, _____ (descriptive word)
_____, _____ (descriptive word)
_____, _____(noun, verb with an *ing* ending)
_____, _____ (noun, verb with an *ing* ending)
_____, _____ (noun, verb with an *ing* ending)
_____ (name or type of snake)

Finally: Students will write their own patterned poems and attach them to the side of the habitat display.

Alternative Assessment: Students will select someone else's snake exhibit and tell the class everything they know about that particular snake and habitat.

Activity 3

Content: Science, Math

Lesson: Comparisons

Standard: Students will identify the basic structures and characteristics of reptiles.

Multiple Intelligence: Logical/Mathematical: Students will create a comparison chart.

Materials: Chart paper, art supplies, butcher paper

Grade Level: 1–3

Objective: The students will research the characteristics of crocodiles and alligators and create a comparison chart of the two. Students will create a mural that includes drawings of both types of reptiles.

Before: Read the chapter on crocodiles and alligators in the book, *Can Snakes Crawl Backwards? Questions and Answers about Reptiles,* by Melvin and Gilda Berger, illustrated by Alan Male (New York: Scholastic, 2001).

First: Students will discuss and list the different physical and habitual characteristics of the two reptiles.

Next: Students will divide into three groups. One group will use information about crocodiles and draw and cut out several crocs. One group will use information about alligators and do likewise. The third group will use information about the habitat of these two reptiles and draw a habitat landscape on a large piece of butcher paper, which will be tacked on a bulletin board.

Then: Students will place their crocs and gators on the mural.

Finally: Students may write a story, fact or fictional, about the whole mural scene.

Alternative Assessment: Students will discuss their own alligator, crocodile, and habitat artwork and point out facts about these representations.

Activity 4

Content: Science

Lesson: Turtles

Standard: Students will identify the basic characteristics and structures of turtles that allow them to live and survive in specific environments. Students will write an informational ad or report.

Multiple Intelligence: Visual/Spatial: Students will construct and paint turtle shells.

Materials: Art supplies, hamburger-type containers

Grade Level: 1–3

Objective: Students will research different types of turtles. Students will compare the shells of these reptiles. Students will use factual information to assist in the construction of these shells.

Before: Bring a turtle into class. Students will observe the turtle's behavior. As the day progresses, students will think of one question they wish to know about that turtle specifically or about turtles in general. At the end of the day, the teacher will lead a discussion using student questions.

First: Read the chapter on turtles in the book, *Can Snakes Crawl Backwards?* Show pictures of turtles from the *Pocket Guide to Familiar Reptiles and Amphibians of North America* and other turtle resource books.

Next: Students will select one turtle and create a representation of the shell of that turtle.

Then: Students will use hamburger-type containers to design and paint the shell of the selected turtle.

Finally: Turtle shells will be exhibited. Students will give a short oral report about each of their turtles and the characteristics of the shells.

Alternative Assessment: Students will create a factual ad for selling their turtles.

Activity 5

Content: Language Arts

Lesson: Creative Writing

Standard: Students will use correct conventions: spelling, punctuation, grammar, word usage, and penmanship.

Multiple Intelligences: Verbal/Linguistic: Students will write a story. Verbal/Spatial: Students will illustrate a story.

Materials: None

Grade Level: 2–4

Objective: Students will use a variety of titles to use as catalysts for writing a creative story or poem, and then illustrate their stories.

Before: Students will create a long sock snake, using many old socks stuffed with newspaper and taped together with duck tape.

First: Read *The Day Jimmy's Boa Ate the Wash,* by Trinka Hakes Noble, illustrated by Steven Kellogg (New York: Scholastic, 1980).

Next: With the teacher's guidance, students will brainstorm other titles or other things the boa might possibly eat. Suggested titles include:

> *The Day Jimmy's Boa Ate the School*
> *The Day Jimmy's Boa Ate the Bicycle*

The Day Jimmy's Boa Ate Disneyland

The Day Jimmy's Boa Ate the RV

The Day Jimmy's Boa Ate the Watermelon

The Day Jimmy's Boa Ate the Baseball Bat

Then: Using the sock snake, and an additional prop that adds to a better understanding of the title, the teacher will arrange a scene with the sock snake and the prop. Each day, the scene and title will change and the children will use these scenes as fifteen-minute writing activities.

Finally: Students create a collection of their writings, illustrate those stories, bind them, and make them into a book.

Alternative Assessment: Another class at the same grade level may wish to write a factual story about why Jimmy's boa couldn't possible eat certain things as mentioned in the creative stories.

Activity 6

Content: Science, Creative Arts

Lesson: Camouflage

Standard: Students will identify the physical characteristics of snakes or other reptiles that allow them to live in specific environments.

Multiple Intelligences: Verbal/Linguistic: Students will research physical aspects of certain snakes. Visual/Spatial: Students will draw a picture.

Materials: Art supplies

Grade Level: 1–3

Objective: Students will draw a camouflage picture.

Before: Students will look around the room for a concealed object that has been camouflaged by the teacher to "disappear" into a certain part of the room. Students will make inferences.

First: Give a short lesson on animals and how they camouflage themselves for survival and adaptability measures.

Next: Read Keith Baker's classic little book, *Hide and Seek* (New York: Harcourt, Brace, 1991). Students will spend time on the illustrations, looking for the hidden snake in each picture.

Then: Students will choose a snake or another reptile and create a drawing that includes a "hidden" or camouflaged reptile.

Finally: Artwork will be displayed on a bulletin board. Students will spend time searching for the hidden reptiles.

Alternative Assessment: Students will write or tell a tale of how a certain reptile got its ability to disappear, change colors, or hide from predators.

Activity 7

Content: Science, Language Arts

Lesson: Factual Poetry

Standards: Students will use reading comprehension strategies. Students will identify characteristics of certain reptiles.

Multiple Intelligences: Verbal/Linguistic: Students will read a poem. Interpersonal: Students will give factual reports.

Materials: Chart paper

Grade Level: 2–3

Objective: The students will read a poem and research information found in the poem for authenticity.

Before: Create a KWL chart about lizards.

First: Put this poem on chart paper. Use as a review, as a phonics lesson on rhyming, as a science resource for children, or simply as a whole group poetry activity.

Lizards

Collared lizards live on rocks
With scales as smooth as glass
And though quite beautiful to see
They bite and hold on fast
And when they hear a little noise
Their back legs make them run
Like little baby dinosaurs
To another pool of sun.

Chuckwallas. What a funny name
Their scales are hot to touch
They eat on food that's mostly green
They don't like meat too much
And when they hear a little noise
They puff up big and fat
And wedge themselves into a crack
Now, what's the sense of that?

The side-blotched lizard can be found
In many sites out West
It has a taste for crawly things
Loves scorpions the best
And when it hears a little noise
The danger is quite real
For other lizards like to make
This one their noonday meal.

The gila monster has sharp teeth
Its scales a crazy quilt
Of black and pink and yellow orange
Its body is strongly built
And when it hears a little noise
It doesn't shake with fright
Because it's usually underground
With thoughts of what to bite.

The little gecko likes the dark
It prowls when stars are out
But in the day it finds a rock
And never roams about
And when it hears a little noise
It curls its tail up high
Or simply snaps his tail right off
As he goes running by.

And last, there is the horny toad
Who dines on big, live ants
And makes his eyelids squirt out blood
If given half a chance
And when he hears a little noise
He never moves away
Because his color blends right in
And where he sits, he'll stay.

Next: Students will read the poem, then look in resource books to find factual information that has been included in the poem.

Then: Students will choose one type of lizard and draw a picture that represents the lizard and one fact.

Finally: Students will share personal stories about lizards they have seen.

Alternative Assessment: Students will write a journal entry about one of the lizards and their fear of or appreciation for a certain type of lizard.

✔ *And now, what about five good lessons from one good book?* See if these work.

The book: Weeks, Sara. Illustrated by Suzanne Duranceau. (1995). *Follow the Moon.* New York: HarperCollins.

1. Students will discuss the point of view from which the book is written.
2. Students will use the website http://cccturtle.org/overview.htm to answer the following questions.
   a. Where do sea turtles live?
   b. Which of the five senses is the best on sea turtles?
   c. How and why were sea turtles exploited?
   d. It is said that sea turtles can live over _____ years.
   e. How old are the earliest known fossils of sea turtles?

      f. The appearance of sea turtles ranges in _____, _____, and _____.

      g. Depending on the species, these turtles can weigh less than _____ pounds and as much as _____ pounds.

      h. What does the scientific name of a turtle identify?

      i. What does the common name describe?

      j. List three common names of turtles.

3. Students will use a Venn diagram to describe the similarities and differences that exist between the real moon and the baby turtle's moon in the story.

4. Students will use clay to create their own turtle friends, which can be placed in a shoe-box lid.

5. Students will write their own endings to the book, *Follow the Moon.*

✎ ***Oh yes. Remember the teachable moment*** that introduced our activities in this chapter? Well, here is a little lesson to go with that idea.

Activity 8

Content: Health and Safety

Lesson: Snakebites

Standard: Students will demonstrate first-aid procedures and responses to common emergencies.

Multiple Intelligences: Bodily/Kinesthetic: Students will role-play scenarios. Interpersonal: Students will teach a first-aid lesson to parents.

Materials: Resource materials

Grade Level: 3

Objective: Students will take a field trip to observe outlying places that may harbor hidden snakes. Students will role-play emergency measures to take when dealing with a snakebite.

Before: Show pictures of poisonous snakes. Discuss the physical characteristics of each.

First: Teach a lesson on types of venom and various ways in which poisonous snakes bite their victims.

Next: Take a field trip around a wooded area. Observe areas where snakes might conceal themselves.

Then: Teach a lesson on snakebite first aid. Students will role-play scenarios.

Finally: Students will choose one aspect of first-aid awareness that has been taught. Students will write or draw a journal entry focusing on that one aspect.

Alternative Assessment: Students will teach this first-aid information to their parents. Parents will respond with some evidence of a lesson learned.

✎ And finally, if you think ***a picture is worth a thousand words,*** use the *Snake* drawing on the next page to engage your students in seeing, writing, drawing, or just thinking about these slithery,

beautiful, extraordinary creatures who seem to scare the pants off of us. The activities surrounding the snake drawing should work wonders for boys and girls who love snakes and who have a clearer understanding of these reptiles if they can learn through color, shape, form, and design.

Activity 9

Content: Language Arts

Lesson: Myths

Standard: Students will write a creative story.

Multiple Intelligence: Visual/Spatial: Students will color a drawing. Verbal/Linguistic: Students will write a story or paragraph.

Materials: Copies of snake drawing

Grade Level: 1–3

Objective: The students will color the snake drawing in an imaginative way and write a myth explaining how the snake got its particular color.

Before: To familiarize students with the origin and importance of myths, legends, and fairy tales in all cultures, read a myth, legend, or fairy tale from one of the following books:

Batt, Tanya Robin, and Gail Newey, illus. *The Child's Book of Fairies*. Cambridge, MA: Barefoot Books, 2002.Dawauendewa, Gerald. *The Butterfly Dance*. New York: Abbeville Press, 2001.

Bennet, J., William, ed., and Michael Hague, illus. *The Children's Book of Heroes*. New York: Simon and Schuster, 1997.

Dawauendewa, Gerald. *The Butterfly Dance*. New York: Abbeville Press, 2001.

Duncan, Lois, and Shonto Begay, illus. *The Magic of Spider Woman*. New York: Scholastic, 1996.

Hague, Michael, ed. and illus. *The Book of Dragons*. New York: William Morrow and Company, 1995.

First: Show an example of the snake drawing that has been colored in an unusual way. Write a short myth that goes with the drawing, and read that as well.

Next: Students will color their own snake drawing and write a short myth accompanying the drawing.

Then: Students will display these writings and drawings on a myth bulletin board that includes other short myths from different cultures.

Finally: Read more myths from various cultures. Students will reflect upon their meaning and similarities to their own lives.

Alternative Assessment: The students and their families will write joint myths of how the children got their names. A discussion will follow focusing on how the boys and girls were actually named.

Activity 10

Content: Science

Lesson: Cause and Effect

Standard: Students will describe and explain cause-and-effect relationships in living systems.

Multiple Intelligence: Visual/Spatial: Students will draw.

Materials: Crayons, markers, art supplies, copies of snake drawing

Grade Level: 3

Objective: Students will draw an unusual habitat on, around, and under the snake in the snake drawing. Students will discuss the causes and effects of these improbable and inappropriate habitats.

Before: Briefly give examples of cause-and-effect situations in nature. Some ideas may include:

1. Forest fire: wildlife
2. Tornado: buildings
3. Flood: homes

First: Discuss various habitats that are appropriate for four different types of snakes: python, sea snake, sidewinder, and water moccasin. Children will offer positive cause-and-effect scenarios as well as negative cause-and-effect scenarios regarding the appropriate and inappropriate habitats for these four reptiles.

Next: Students will look at a snake drawing copy. They will think of habitats for this particular snake that might be appropriate or not. Students will draw those habitats around, below, to the side of, and underneath the snake in the picture.

Then: Students will teach the class the causes and effects of having snakes live in these particular environments or habitats. A suggestion is that children initially give some facts about their particular snake drawing: where it might actually live, what it might eat, how it might bear its young, and so on. The habitats drawn may correlate with the facts or not. The correlation or noncorrelation will coincide directly with the cause-and-effect information the children share about the habitats.

Finally: Students will reflect upon their own "habitats," and specific causes and effects that arise from living in those human habitats.

Alternative Assessment: Children will make a comparison chart between their own habitats and those of the snakes they drew.

Activity 11

Content: Language Arts

Lesson: Telling Stories

Standard: Students will use effective vocabulary and organization to relate information.

Multiple Intelligences: Visual/Spatial: Students will use the snake drawing as a stimulus for telling a story. Verbal/Linguistic: Students will tell a story. Intrapersonal: Students will reflect upon past experiences.

Materials: Copies of the snake drawing

Grade Level: K–3

Objective: Students will look at the different elements of the drawing in this chapter and tell an original story.

Before: Students will review important aspects of telling a story.

First: Students will use the snake drawing as a stimulus for telling stories about different experiences happening in the scenes in the picture.

Next: Students will relate personal stories that correspond to the original stories being told.

Then: Students will answer "What would happen if . . . " questions about the picture.

Finally: Students will reflect upon their own appreciation of the drawing.

Alternative Assessment: Students will take a drawing home and ask a family member to tell them a story that comes from viewing the drawing.

So, here is every idea you ever wanted to know about snakes and other crawly things. Wiggle these toward your students and see what happens.

Snakes and Other Crawly Things K–3

V/L	Find a children's book about snakes that is based on fiction.	Research the different markings of snakes.	Write a "ten best things snakes do" list.	Write a "ten worst things snakes do" list.	Read *The Day Jimmy's Boa Ate the Wash*. "Talk" fact and fiction.
L/M	Use math and reasoning skills to make it factual.	Create a graph of snake characteristics.	Create "What if" questions about snakes.	Create habitats for this snake. Make some predictions.	Create a logical ending to this story.
V/S	Design a long snake using toilet paper rolls connected by string.	Collect small sticks. Paint and design them in same design as a snake studied.	With help from an upper grade, create a snake exhibit.	Illustrate an ABC book of snakes.	Look at several books on snakes. Observe different illustrations.
B/K	Construct the snake and habitat that goes with it.	Act out this story verbally and nonverbally.	Create movement sequences to explain the differences.	Create a snake dance.	Take a field trip around the school. Look for crawly things.
M/R	Find and sing songs about snakes.	Create appropriate sound effects that complement these stories.	Play musical chairs with snake fact questions.	Make up your own lyrics.	Create a chant from this information.
Inter	Teach the class about one thing you learned from the illustrations.	Go into another class and share your findings.	Use interactive software regarding snakes and crawly things.	Volunteer to bring an reptile expert to class.	Brainstorm ways to be on the lookout for snakes while hiking or camping.
Intra	"Snakes scare me because _____."	Create an interest center focusing on your favorite aspect of snakes.	Do an independent study about your favorite snake.	Keep a journal account of this care.	"If I were a snake, the one thing I would change about me is _____."
N	Research the tasks of herpetologist.	Research and compare common adaptability characteristics among certain snakes.	Take care of it for a week.	Create a food chain pertaining to certain crawly things.	How do the illustrated environments make sense?

The activities and experiences in this grid are just a bit more difficult and can bring some challenges to your students. These ideas can be used as extension lessons or individual projects, or, in some cases, in learning centers.

Snakes and Other Crawly Things 4–6

V/L	Research ten different crawly things.	Write an original myth of why snakes have no legs. Script it.	Investigate snakes and their connection to cultural customs.	Write a story about a crawly thing. Leave out all adjectives.	Create a crawly thing dictionary.
L/M	Create a timeline of snakes and historical significance.	Compare the myths for similarities.	Chart the findings.	Other students will problem solve appropriate adjectives to go with the stories.	Compare potency of venom among poisonous crawly things.
V/S	Design a geography board from information about these crawly things.	Ask first-graders to illustrate the crawly thing dictionary with you.	Design a container for a specific crawly thing.	Draw appropriate habitats for five global crawly things.	Draw illustrations for the crawly thing dictionary.
B/K	Create a mini-play from the script.	Play each other's board games. Use this as a review.	Create a puppet play from the rewritten script.	Create a three-dimensional representation of your story.	Research authentic snake dances of other cultures. Learn one.
M/R	Use recorders to play improvised music appropriate to some of these cultural customs.	Select ten facts about snakes. Create a rap from these facts.	Write a song about these myths.	Collect and sing songs about snakes or crawly things.	Create a snake hand-jive using these facts.
Inter	In groups, rewrite Keith Baker's book, *Hide and Seek*.	Volunteer to write zoos. Gather information about the caring of pets in a zoo environment.	Use online information to present a report to the class about snakes.	Interview snake owners.	Lead a discussion on the myths around snakes.
Intra	Do an independent study on how the snake is used in advertisements.	Collect and/or create metaphors for "snake."	Why do snakes get such a bad rap?	If you had to eat a snake to survive, would you be able to? Why or why not?	Write a journal entry about your phobia of snakes.
N	Investigate natural habitats of venomous crawly things.	Research and discuss antivenom medicines.	Connect snakes to medicine in general, past and present.	Investigate the evolution of snakes and other crawly things.	Investigate species that are now extinct.

Index

Martha Brady is a national educational consultant and the author of *Dancing Hearts: Creative Arts with Books Kids Love, Artstarts, Using Multiple Intelligence Strategies to Improve Student Learning, Integrating Creative Arts throughout Your Program,* and a cassette of songs for children, *Smart Pets.* She is on the faculty of Northern Arizona University in Flagstaff, Arizona.

Michele Edwards, born and raised in Detroit, now lives in the Boston area. She is known locally for her finely detailed landscape and architectural drawings. This is her first publication, which she dedicates to her father.

www.ingramcontent.com/pod-product-compliance
Lightning Source LLC
Chambersburg PA
CBHW080421270326
41929CB00018B/3114